THE STORY OF THE 2/5th BATTALION
THE GLOUCESTERSHIRE REGIMENT
1914–1918

WAR MEMORIAL.
The Public Park, Gloucester.

THE STORY OF THE
2/5th BATTALION
GLOUCESTERSHIRE
REGIMENT
1914-1918

Edited by

A. F. BARNES, M.C.

B.A., MUS. DOC. (OXON)., F.R.C.O.
HON. A.R.C.M. (CAPTAIN, O.C. "C"
COMPANY AND ACTING ADJUTANT).

GLOUCESTER
THE CRYPT HOUSE PRESS, LIMITED
1930

EDITOR'S PREFACE

An Editor's task is never a simple one ; in the present instance it has been more than ordinarily difficult for a variety of reasons.

In the first place, owing to the enthusiasm for the Battalion and the desire to have its story in print, an enormous number of letters, diaries and reminiscences have been collected. Often these are of too personal a nature to be suitable, many of them overlap as regards dates, some are inaccurate as to facts while there are sometimes wide discrepancies between two accounts of the same episode.

Secondly, many writers quite naturally fall into the error of recording events from the point of view of the particular section or part of the Battalion to which they belonged rather than of the unit as a whole.

A third difficulty lies in the fact that in no instance has the manuscript been accompanied by a map of any description. It is true that a certain number of maps appear in the book, but these were not obtained without much searching and delay : meanwhile the book had to be compiled without them.

There were other minor obstacles such as illegibility to be overcome, but the above were the main difficulties that faced me when I was asked to undertake the editing of this Journal.

After a close perusal of all the material, I have had to consider how it could best be used for the purpose in hand. The conclusions which I have arrived at will be understood, if I set down the principles upon which I have worked and what the carrying out of those principles has involved.

The story is told in narrative form, and in order to preserve homogeneity it is told in the third person. Thus personal diaries have been largely remoulded, much of a too personal nature has been omitted, and only by way of occasional quotations have parts of them been used in their original form.

As the volume purports to be a story of the Battalion, the Battalion has been the focus round which persons and events move. This has entailed the ruthless omission of a large amount of material centring round companies and sections, where I feel that its inclusion is in danger of contravening Euclid's axiom that the part should never be greater than the whole.

Moreover, such a narrative as this should be a human document rather than a technical treatise on military operations. I have, therefore, included anecdotes wherever possible and have excluded matter of a technical nature such as operation orders or the dispositions of other units, except where such facts have a bearing on the activities of the 2/5th Glosters.

For the bare facts of the narrative, I have relied almost entirely on the notes of Lt.-Col. the Hon. A. B. Bathurst, Lt.-Col. G. F. Collett, D.S.O., Lt.-Col. G. C. Christie Miller, D.S.O., M.C., Capt. L. Dudbridge, M.C., Capt. R. S. B. Sinclair, M.C., Capt. H. V. Gray, M.C., Sgt. R. J. Child, Sgt. Clare, Cpl. Little, Rev. J. Partum Milum—together with correspondence of Brig.-Gen. the Hon. Robert White, supplied by Major Rickerby, and Capt. M. Badcock's diary, supplied by Mrs. Badcock. I would ask all the above contributors to accept this mention as an earnest of my sense of indebtedness to them.

My thanks are also due to Brig.-Gen. A. W. Pagan, Major Rickerby for various correspondence connected with Capt. Rickerby, his son, Major G. L. Day, Capt. and Q.M. Tomlins, Lieut. F. W. Harvey for notes on his brother, as well as to Sgt. A. T. Voyce, Sgt. Greening, Sgt. E. G. White, Sgt. H. F. Terrett, Sgt. H. Webb, Sgt. C. Dobbs, Q.M.S. Gilbert, Ptes. C. J. Horlick, S. Palmer, A. W. Lewis,

EDITOR'S PREFACE

G. Winfield. The material of these contributors either duplicates other accounts, or is too diffuse to form the basis of any one chapter : it has, therefore, been utilised piecemeal wherever a paragraph lends colour to the *mise-en-scène* of the story and for testing the accuracy of other contributions : in both respects it has been of the utmost value.

A further debt of gratitude is due to Major the Rt. Hon. C. P. Allen for photographs, to Lt.-Col. Christie Miller and Capt. John Hunter for the loan of maps and suggestions and to the members of the Executive Committee (Lt.-Col. G. F. Collett, Capt. L. Dudbridge, Sgt. E. C. Gibbs and Sgt. J. H. Gurney) for their unstinted support and encouragement.

This is not the place to apologise for the way in which I have mutilated the contributions submitted to my judgment, for this, I understand, is the prerogative of an Editor, but I do feel that I ought to plead some defence for such inaccuracies and omissions as are almost bound to occur in a journal compiled in this way. May I, therefore, remind readers that I was not with the Battalion during a considerable part of its sojourn in France and ask them also to remember that, after a lapse of years, memory is at best an unreliable ally.

It has, however, been said somewhere that the best history of Oxford was written by a lady who had spent one day in Cambridge. While the stimulus to essay my task has been this assurance, the urge to complete it has been the opportunity it gives me of recording the ungarbled facts in the life of the normal soldier, facts distorted by none of the exaggerations and abnormalities that some recent books have taught the public to associate with the fighting men. This is a story of plain men, who fought because they hated war, who voluntarily sacrificed themselves for their country and their friends and in the doing of it, lost not their humour, their standard of duty, nor their faith.

A. F. BARNES.

CONTENTS

MAPS

ILLUSTRATIONS

ILLUSTRATIONS

FOREWORD

BY

MAJOR-GENERAL SIR COLIN MACKENZIE,

K.C.B., C.B., ETC.

General Officer Commanding 61st Division 1915–1918.
Colonel of the Seaforth Highlanders.

This history of the 2/5th Gloucester Regiment is written with a restraint and a dignity worthy and typical of its character, and its grand record in the Great War. It is a simple and truthful account of devoted service, rendered with heroic spirit and steadfast courage.

The 2/5th Glosters during the war showed they possessed in a high degree the qualities of their county ; qualities which are of the essence of the real England ; steady, deep and true ; and under the leadership of Colonels of special distinction the Battalion went surely forward, from good to better, with a quiet and growing confidence in itself which nothing checked or daunted.

A Divisional Commander is perhaps not in such close and frequent touch with any particular battalion as its Brigadier, but he is sufficiently so to know much more about it than he is sometimes given credit for. At any rate, I may say, as commanding the Division, that I knew the 2/5th Glosters very well, and their Colonels, and valued them accordingly. I always had confidence that they would carry out any task given them if humanly possible, and my confidence was rewarded in many dark days and dubious issues. In reading their story this comes freshly back to my mind, and I tender them anew my gratitude and respect.

1st September, 1930.

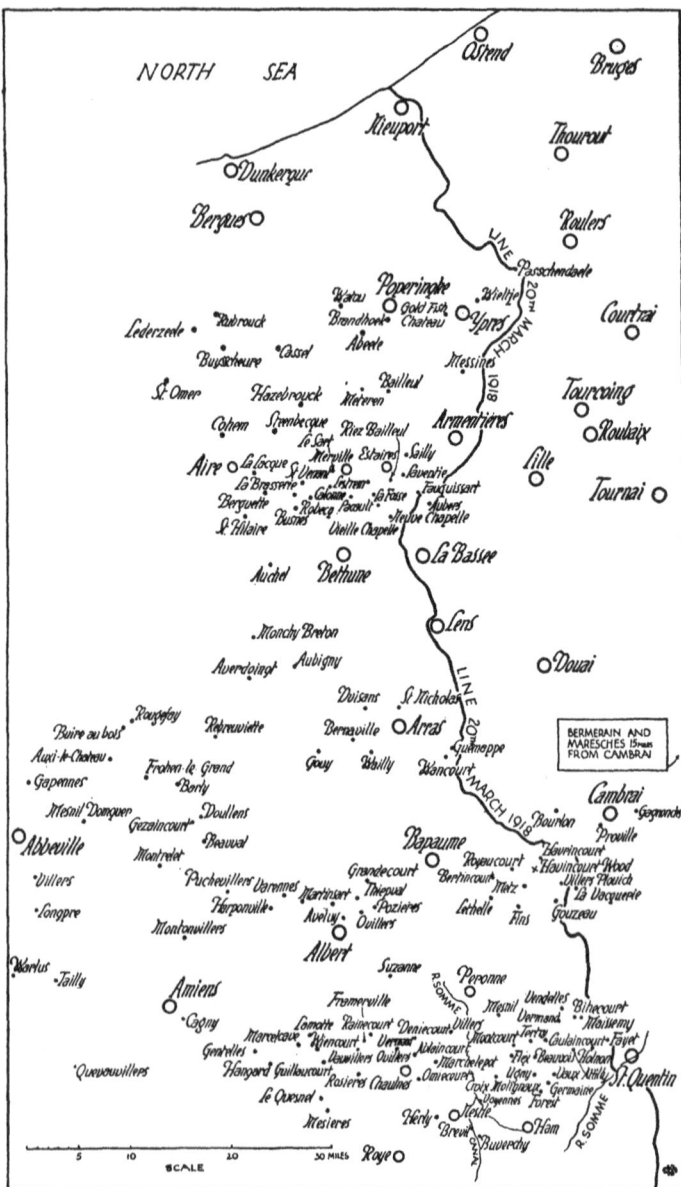

General Map showing Locality
and Places visited by Battalion.

OFFICERS—GLOUCESTER, 1914.

The Story of the 2/5th Battalion The Gloucestershire Regiment 1914-1918

CHAPTER I

EARLY DAYS—GLOUCESTER TO SALISBURY PLAIN

THE war had not been in progress many weeks before the necessity for sending Territorial units overseas became obvious. So it was in the early part of September 1914 that the 2/5th Battalion of the Gloucestershire Regiment came into being to act as a second line to the 1/5th already in existence. Lt.-Col. the Hon. A. B. Bathurst was asked to raise and to command the new unit, designated at the time, a Home Service Battalion.

The task of forming the new unit was a formidable one, since there was not only no personnel, but there was also no working machinery upon which to build it up.

The first step in this direction was taken when several officers were sent back from the first line to serve at the Depot in Gloucester. Included in this number were Major S. S. Champion, Major E. G. Moore and Major the Rt. Hon. C. P. Allen, all of whom had a considerable experience of territorial soldiering behind them ; the latter two remained with the Battalion during the time it was being trained into a fighting unit and both were of the utmost value in its formation and in its subsequent development.

The 1/5th also provided the new Battalion with its two most essential functionaries in R.S.M. Tomlins and Q.M.S. Canavan.

With this nucleus of officers and warrant officers at his back, Lt.-Col. Bathurst was able to devote his attentions to enlisting the services of a capable Adjutant and Quartermaster, the latter at the moment being the more urgent.

Mr. Oswald Harrison, a man of wide commercial experience, who had lately come to live at Cirencester, was approached on the matter. After due consideration he consented to take the post, with the modest comment that he would do his best. It was no small sacrifice for a man of middle age, and, judged by ordinary standards, one well furnished with worldly goods, to give up the life of a leisured gentleman for the arduous duties of a Battalion Quartermaster. Nevertheless Lt. Harrison or the " old Q.M." as he came to be called by his brother officers, was a conspicuous success not only because of his business acumen but also because of his social charm, his tact and his generosity. His death some few years after the war came as a real blow to those whom he had served so well.

Recruiting was by this time in full swing and the numbers mounted rapidly. No uniforms were available, so the men were paraded and drilled in all sorts of civilian attire, each man wearing a square of white silk on the lapel of his coat inscribed with the words 2/5th Glosters to show that he had joined up. Some, like C.Q.M.S. Roberts, appeared on parade as recruits minus hats, until a Battalion order saying that all N.C.O.'s and men must wear head-dress, compelled them to renounce the fashion.

It was exceedingly interesting to watch the gradual transformation from mufti to khaki and the other various stages of progress through which, out of its raw beginnings, an admirable battalion was ultimately and speedily formed. It was a proud day indeed when it was strong enough to march from barracks to Oxleaze for battalion drill, and a paying day for the proprietors of the Palladium when they were able to show a film featuring the Battalion on the march.

The City of Gloucester, under the auspices of its Mayor,

Mr. (now Sir) James Bruton, showed every kindness and consideration to both officers and men. The early days in Gloucester were thus made as pleasant as possible. An officers' mess was provided at the Gloucester Club, an act of hospitality on the part of the City which was most acceptable, and the mess remained there until it was eventually moved in December to the Judge's Lodgings. The men were billetted in the City.

Early in January 1915, a draft from the 2nd line was sent to Chelmsford. About this time also the Marquis of Salisbury was appointed as Divisional General and Col. Ludlow as Brigade Commander, the 2/5th becoming one of the units within these organisations.

On February 1st the Battalion left the hospitable City of Gloucester for Northampton, the assembling point of the whole division. What a wrench it must have been for the men to leave behind for good and all the Monk's Retreat can best be appreciated by the fact that for months, nay, years afterwards, their simple hearts responded to its memories. Whether foot-slogging along a dusty road or trudging up the line, they would sing about that mysterious rendezvous. The tune, it is true, began to cloy in course of time, but the words, which told of the pomegranates and melons, among other things, that grew there, made those who joined the Battalion after its Gloucester days, wonder if they had not missed the best part of the war.

Northampton gave the men their first experience of being billetted in a strange Borough : it also afforded the Battalion its first lessons in training as a part of a large unit.

While at Northampton, Lt.-Col. Bathurst met with a riding accident, which resulted in a broken collar bone, but otherwise no casualties occurred.

The usual routine of Divisional, Brigade and Battalion training was carried on without incident ; but many will remember a surprise night alarm which, owing to a highly organised intelligence system, did not take the Glosters unawares, as it was expected to do. At night, entertainments of various kinds were organised. One concert, at which Mr. Gervase Elwes delighted his audience by his beautiful voice, stands out in particular.

From Northampton, the Battalion proceeded to Chelmsford in April, the Division being distributed in the neighbourhood around that town.

Here further stages of training were carried out. Kit inspections recurred with irritating regularity : they became the Q.M.'s favourite hobby and the men became experts in passing mess tin covers from the rear to the front rank and back again without being observed by the officer looking for shortages.

A new experience to many was provided by the Musketry practices which were fired at this time. The firing took place at Boreham—and it did. The level of the shooting was surprisingly high until the dodge of sticking pencils through the targets was discovered.

It was while at Chelmsford that many of the new officers took the opportunity of becoming more closely acquainted with the art of equestration. The transport officer, Lieut. Cyril Cole, provided an assortment of mounts for them, including race horses, cab horses and mules. One horse in particular, " Old Tom," earned the affectionate regard of the nervous rider, because of his leisurely habits. He had been employed in a milk float and true to his pre-war training, he stopped automatically at every gate, an act of grace, which allowed his rider to regain the stirrups without any apparent loss of dignity. Poor old Tom ! only once in his life was he known to hurry. It was during a battalion drill : companies were marching in open column and Tom was in a place of honour leading the third Company. Suddenly the order rang out, " Battalion, form close column of companies." The officer cradled on Tom's ample back shouted, " C Company double march." No double marching for me, thought Tom : he was thinking perhaps of what might happen to the milk.

The result was that the flanks doubled forward, while the centre of the line was kept back by the imperturbable Tom. The Company thus proceeded in a semi-circular formation until a resourceful N.C.O. prodded him with a bayonet. Then it was that Tom awoke to the " stern " realities of the situation and actually trotted forward for the first and only time in his recorded existence.

There was an occasion too at Chelmsford when, in the absence of Captain Ash, the Commanding Officer asked Lieut. Seymour Tubbs to act as his adjutant on a certain Divisional field day. Lt.-Col. Bathurst had some doubts as to Seymour Tubbs' capacities as a horseman, but he was assured by him that though he could not ride much, he was willing to try. Accordingly the quietest horse was given him for the day. Alas ! in the course of the proceedings, a charger dashed by the C.O. with an empty saddle and a minute or two later, a General Staff Officer came up with the information that the acting adjutant of the 2/5th Glosters was reposing unhurt in a hedge some distance up the road.

An important branch of training at this time took the form of night operations. No doubt these operations were designed with a view to giving the higher command experience in organisation and general staff duties : it is quite certain that the rank and file had not the smallest conception what they were doing or why they were doing it. From time to time, however, something happened that afforded a fund of amusement. One night, when the Brigade was on the march to night operations, the 2/5th Glosters happened to be the leading Battalion. The night was pitch black and the road was little more than a lane with a ditch on either side, when the Brigade ordered a halt. There was no place where the men could sit down, so they merely loosened belts and remained standing roughly in column of fours. Then the fun began. One of the mules at the rear of the Battalion started to scratch the ground, causing a noise that certainly sounded like the clatter of several hooves. "A stampede" was the thought that electrified everyone. There was a general surge forward from the rear and in far less time than it takes to tell the road was clear and the entire personnel of the gallant 2/5th was struggling in the two ditches, an inconceivable tangle of men, rifles and equipment. Rumour has it that the Brigadier was pushed into one ditch and the Brigade Major into the other, but this has not been sub-stantiated. All that can be said for certain is that the Brigade Major's gift for trenchant language was not affected by the incident, though there were some who thought it would have been fairer had he expended some of his in-vective on the unsuspecting mule who was the cause of all the trouble.

During the summer months of 1915 Zeppelins made frequent raids to this country and occasionally passed over Chelmsford, but only on two occasions were bombs actually dropped on the town. The Battalion's interest in the Zeppelin scare lay in the provision of what was called an aeroplane picquet. The picquet consisted of an officer and some twenty-five to thirty men : this party marched a few miles out of Chelmsford and took up its position after dusk in a quarry. The picquet was connected by telephone with Brigade and was armed with Japanese rifles : two or three sentries were posted, who watched motor car head-lights on distant roads and liked to imagine that they were flash-light signals made by evilly disposed Germans. Thus the night wore on and after an early breakfast, the party marched back to Chelmsford to be off duty for the remainder of the day. In the words of Col. Bathurst, it is a little difficult to understand what possible use a man with a rifle could be against an airship, and in the light of present day experience it seems almost incredible that the idea of mounting such a picquet should ever have been entertained.

From Chelmsford the Battalion went to Epping for several weeks where its main occupation was work on the

LT.-COL. THE HON. A. B. BATHURST.
Commanding Officer, September 1914—March 1916.

trench system that formed part of the outer defences of London.

Returning again to Chelmsford, the Division was inspected by Earl Kitchener.

Moving back to Epping a little later, the Battalion went under canvas, and then towards the end of the year it returned to Chelmsford where it remained until February 1916, when the Division moved to Salisbury Plain for the final stages of its training for active service overseas.

" The arrival on Salisbury Plain," writes Col. Bathurst, " was signalised by wintry conditions. On detraining, at Tidworth, the village was found enveloped in deep snow and a biting wind was blowing : we were soon made to realise that however warm the Plain may be in summer, it was an exceedingly chilly spot in a hard winter. I look back on those days at Gloucester, Northampton, Chelmsford, Epping and Salisbury Plain with some sadness mingled with a pardonable pride—sadness because I knew that the command of the Battalion would have to pass into other hands when the time came for it to go overseas—pride in the contemplation of a Battalion evolved out of a heterogeneous collection of recruits, lacking rifles, uniforms and every other essential and shaped into a fighting unit fit for any call that may be made upon it, and destined to fulfil its rôle with no small measure of distinction. My keen regret in parting from the Battalion was mollified by the reflection that I had done my best to discharge the duty committed to me in humble devotion to the public need."

Lt.-Col. Bathurst had good reason to be proud of his achievement, for with the help of a mere handful of others he had raised the battalion : he had got together a splendid body of officers and men and endowed them with an enthusiasm, which helped them to carry on the great traditions of the Gloucestershire Regiment.

CHAPTER II

ON SALISBURY PLAIN

On the night of February 19th, the Battalion reached Tidworth and marched to its quarters at Parkhouse Camp, there being met by Capt. Beloe who afterwards became Adjutant. First impressions of life on the Plain were not very encouraging : the weather was bitterly cold ; there were no palliasses ; there were no fires and no light as the electricity failed on the night of the Battalion's arrival. The men were put into huts, given rations and three blankets apiece and left to get what sleep they could on bare bed boards.

On the following morning they awoke or it would be truer to say, arose, since sleep under such circumstances was a sheer impossibility, to find a blizzard of snow and sleet blowing gaily. The day was spent in improving huts, on lighting and relighting recalcitrant stoves, unpacking kit and so forth. By the following day, the Battalion had so far settled down that the Brigadier was able to inspect it.

On the 22nd a further inspection was made by Sir John French.

Here are Capt. Badcock's words : " At 1.30 we marched out of huts and were drawn up on the hill side ; snow was falling and a perishing gale blew : we stood for nearly two hours frozen to the marrow. Sir John French came round at 3.20 p.m. and had a look at us. He was a small man with a white moustache and red face : he wore a big fur coat which hid most of him. After Sir John French had departed, Brig.-Col. Ludlow bade us farewell as Gen. Fortesque was about to take over command of the Brigade."

Capt. Badcock goes on to give an instance of a hut orderly's somewhat acid sense of humour. "I made," he writes, "some rather caustic remarks about a pat of rancid butter that had been left in one of the huts by the outgoing troops and had not been removed by our fellows. 'We kept it, Sir,' the orderly explained, 'because we don't want, in these margarine days, to forget what real butter looks like.'"

Intensively cold weather continued to prevail, but Capt. Badcock records that on the night of the 24th he spent his first warm night, so it is safe to assume that by then the life of the men as a whole was becoming more comfortable.

Naturally, as the Plain was the stepping off place for overseas, training took a much more practical form. Lieut. Graydon, M.O., lectured the troops on hygiene and field dressings : Lieut. Bernard initiated them into the mysteries of bombs and detonators ; Lieut. Wales of the Lincolns, who had already been wounded and evacuated, imparted to the officers all the latest information about trench digging and devices for fire steps, cover, listening posts and other things. Thus the days passed by. A thaw set in on March 1st, rain began to fall and very soon the Plain was transformed into a quagmire of mud and slush.

About this time the Battalion went through another course of musketry practices. The weather was still bitterly cold and those long trudges over broken ground to the butts, the everlasting " Port Arms," the discouraging " Washout " signal are among the episodes of war which everyone tries to forget.

March 9th was a field day. At the close of the operation the men and kit were inspected, and later on the same day Lieut.-Col. Bathurst bade farewell to the Battalion, handing over the reins to Major Percy Balfour, who arrived the following day.

Rumours of all sorts began to float around ; first it was

that the Brigadier was getting authority for the Battalion to wear the back badge : then it was that the Division was going to France on May 1st ; it even was current that two German Cruisers had been sunk on Salisbury Plain. All this led to a vast amount of surmise and helped to lighten the monotony of musketry, field days and kit inspections.

The new Commanding Officer was nothing, if not a hustler. His strong points were organisation and interior economy, and in these respects he certainly added enormously to the efficiency of the Battalion and gave it just that precision and attention to detail that are needed, if the machinery controlling a large body of men is to work smoothly under actual fighting conditions. He made several alterations in the personnel of the Battalion ; Capt. Ash went sick and Capt. Gilbert Beloe became Adjutant ; and a newly joined officer from a cyclist Battalion took over command of C Company from Capt. Barnes.

Lieut. Wales, in company with other officers, sited trenches about this time and from the end of March till the departure for France, the main part of the training consisted of digging and manning trenches. A competition in the gentle art of shovelling mud and chalk was held in which A Company proved the winner.

When a complete trench system had been evolved, exercises were carried out in all the then known branches of trench warfare. Interspersed with these activities were occasional field days and route marches.

One particular field day will always be remembered because of its somewhat obvious unreality. The objective of the attack was some rising ground a few miles from Parkhouse that went by the name of Silk Hill. To the Glosters was accorded the honour of leading the assault, an honour less appreciated later on and often described in different language.

The day was ridiculously hot for the time of year and the perspiring troops, as they trudged up to the foot of the hill, and then extending, advanced up its slopes in short rushes, evinced a wide range of epithets on temperature in general. When they were half way up the hill, the Brigade Major rode up and announced that the hill had been captured. The victorious troops straightway lay down where they stood, serenely oblivious to a possible counter-attack or to the necessity of consolidating their position. To add further absurdity to the situation, an enterprising old market woman from Tidworth strolled round the line, exchanged friendly greetings with the men and sold a large number of oranges. Such was the first occasion upon which the men of the 2/5th tasted the "fruit of victory."

Major Balfour, being a musketry expert, organised a rapid loading competition about this time. The competition took place on March 24th and was won by C Company.

April arrived and every form of practical training became more intensive.

Capt. Badcock went sick about this time. There is a very human touch about his diary that makes it worth quoting:

"On April 7th I got leave and went home. I spent a very jolly time playing tennis and golf, but like all pleasant things it came to an end and I returned to camp on the 13th. The hardest part of all was the saying of good-byes to the family. I think everyone was fine over it. Of course I was not starting for France, but though I did not say so, I knew pretty well that this was the last time I should see them all for some time. This is a beastly war for everyone, but I think the hardest lot is borne by those left behind, who have relatives abroad. For the one who goes abroad, there is the excitement; he is taking part in the Great Adventure; he has time to think neither of danger nor discomfort. For those at home it is so different; they have more spare time to think and fear; they only see the casualty lists in the papers and read about the horrors of trenches and internment camps; they see men come back shattered in body and·listen to the stories they have to tell. How can people at home expect to be cheerful?

No ! the hardest part certainly falls on those who cannot fight, but must wait—and though it does not séem a very heroic rôle, surely it is the greater sacrifice and yet one which the women of England seem fully capable of making, more honour to them."

Capt. Badcock had a long association with the Battalion ; he was a very efficient and enthusiastic officer ; his healthy outlook on life and his cheerful disposition endeared him to both officers and men. He lost his life near Rosieres on March 27th, 1918, at the age of twenty-two.

The above thoughts, expressed with a simplicity so characteristic, have a pathetic significance for those who served with and under him.

Trench fighting and bombing practice continued to be the order of the day, and on April 19th there was a fearsome Divisional Route March of twenty something miles. The 2/5th acquitted itself with distinction and received a complimentary note from the Division.

After returning from this route march, little rest was in store for the Battalion, for after a few hours of comparative idleness, it was dragged out the same night to complete the trenches, in readiness for their occupation the following day.

"This trench digging," Capt. Badcock writes, "is an overrated amusement. One crawls up a very steep hill with a very large spade. The climb alone is hard work, but nothing to what happens at the top. An icy blast, coming straight from the pole, beats upon you ; your hat flies off and is not recaptured until it is arrested half way down the hill by a private who impales it with a pick. Forewarned is forearmed. You ascend the hill again with your chin straps down and after battling against the elements, you reach the crest and behold a dreary-looking incision on the bosom of Mother Earth. You drop in and commence trying to deepen it, with the chalk dust blowing in your eyes. You are probably provided only with a pick and so you are unable to shift the soil you may have

RECRUITS—GLOUCESTER 1914.

LATER—1915.

loosened. You try to bale it out with your hands and then a cheery friend offers to lend you his aid. While you continue to pick up the bits of loose chalk, he nearly amputates your hands with his shovel. This sort of thing continues until your misery is ended by the wailing blast of what at first sounds like the lament of a lost soul, but is in fact the singularly discordant notes of the C.O.'s whistle. Consolation comes, however, on returning to camp and having a warm meal, then sleeping like the proverbial top and waking up ready to do the same thing again."

There is an old saying that if you make a bed, you must lie on it. To parody the proverb—if you dig trenches, you must live in them. And so on the night April 20/21, the Battalion spent its existence in the trenches it had dug with so much perspiration, blistered hands and bad language.

Good Friday and Easter Day came and went very much like any other day.

On April 26th there was a Brigade attack of Quarley Hill. This was the day when the authorities got a scare about the bombardment of Lowestoft. The Battalion was under orders to move at eight hours' notice, ammunition was served out and a pitched battle was thought to be imminent. Nothing came of the excitement, however, and on the following days the troops lapsed into the usual routine of training again.

On May 5th, the Division turned out in full strength to be inspected by His Majesty The King.

"We marched off," says Capt. Badcock, "at 9 a.m. It was close and muggy, but rain during the previous night had laid the dust. As the inspection had been well organised, it was not so long drawn out as most operations of a similar nature. It was a most impressive sight. Twenty thousand men, hundreds of horses and wagons all moving together in an endless line, under the command of a single man—all very fine, fixed bayonets, drawn swords, and bands playing. One does not wish to be a pessimist, but I could not help wondering how many would come back alive from France. The whole mass rolling forward looks irresistible. I have never before taken part in a review on this scale. As we went by, there were scores of pretty girls and smart motors. I wonder if they realised how much extra work this show meant to us—how we had been up and about since 4.30 a.m., had marched nine miles carrying 70 lbs. on our backs—and did they realise that we should get nothing to eat except hard biscuits until 4.30 p.m. . . ."

The two following days were spent in lectures and loafing, two of the " 'ells " in a soldier's life. Then followed a big Brigade operation which lasted three days, starting on May 8th. The Battalion marched 15 miles to Andover and then on to Hurstbourne, where some of the men were billetted and the rest bivouaced. It poured with rain and everyone and everything got soaked. As Battalion Headquarters ran out of bread, Capt. Badcock and Lieut. Hunter were sent out to scour for more. With the instinct of true soldiers, they descended upon a Mrs. Diggle and purchased every crumb of bread she possessed. Even the knowledge that the Brigadier was billetted on her did not melt their martial hearts. On the second day the Battalion marched ten miles to Fullerton, where barns were requisitioned for billetting purposes. At 2 a.m. on the third day, the troops were again on the move, and were pushed on towards Quarley Hill. An attack on Cholderton Hill had just started, when, to use Capt. Badcock's words, the balloon went up. The Battalion closed and marched home.

The next few days passed without incident, but even during these strenuous days a good deal of time was found for innocent amusement. Of one such episode, Capt. Badcock writes : " In the evening we went to a concert given by the Jesters, and afterwards invited them to dinner. Later in the evening, I pretended to be tight and insisted on sleeping in the Imbo's bed. They were fearfully piqued when, after kicking about and snorting, I suddenly jumped up, bade them good-night and walked off : they were really beautifully had. I played the same trick on three more " Cubys," meeting with huge success, except in one case, where a bucket of cold water was resorted to as a means of sobering me. I think camp life, living always among men, and getting no leave, coarsens one, and gives one's wits, jokes and conversation a somewhat dull tone."

The naïve sentiments of the final sentences are delightfully expressive of the healthy-minded British schoolboy. Nothing further worthy of record occurred during the Battalion's remaining days on Salisbury Plain.

Providence has endowed mankind with a wonderful power of adaptability. The Battalion had arrived on the Plain under the worst possible conditions, but despite the discomforts and the tedium of training, Parkhouse Camp had quickly become its home, and though doubtless no one was sorry for a change of venue, yet when the day of departure arrived, there was a feeling of reluctance to leave the Plain and the memories it held in its undulating folds.

Chapter III

DEPARTURE FROM SALISBURY PLAIN

It is little wonder that poets so often sing about the month of May, " when Spring all clad in gladness doth laugh at Winter's sadness." The sun is warm and kindly ; the breezes mellow ; the streams in tiny cascades wend their way over shoal and withy ; the young foliage throws its light shadows over the meadow ; the downland is lush and in the hedgerows Nature's feathered choristers carol.

It dawned such a day when the Battalion left Salisbury Plain for France. It was May 24th, 1916. Everyone was early afoot—there was an atmosphere of excitement about and the Camp presented an unusually spick and span appearance. A move was taking place.

A bugle sounded the " fall in." Men and officers came tumbling out of huts on to the parade ground, laden with the accoutrements of war. The anticipation of a change and the feeling of a new importance made them unconscious of their resemblance to well-stocked Christmas trees. Ranks were dressed, rolls were checked and then the troops stood easy waiting for the moment of departure.

The routine remark, " All present and correct, sir," broke the spell. Many a time before the same words had been uttered, but now they seemed to bear a new significance. Who, it was wondered, would be present when the roll was called on some not far distant date ? What names would fall on ears so deaf that not even the sternest command would rouse them to respond ?

There was a little shuffling, a little adjustment and then

32

came an unemotional " Move to the right in fours." Rifles were sloped in as orthodox a manner as bulging haversacks, dangling ration bags, gas masks, map cases, revolver holsters and a host of other equipment would permit, and so the Battalion marched away. None will forget the figure of C Company's late Commander—Major Allen—who, on the score of age, had not been allowed to go overseas with the Battalion. It must have been a bitter blow to him to have been thus left behind ; it was no less bitter for those who had served with and under him to have to part. He had been with the Battalion since its birth and had come to be regarded as one of its institutions. He combined the qualities of a wise counsellor, a just censor and a generous friend in an unusual degree. His breadth of view, his understanding of men and his discretion brought him into direct sympathy with everyone and played a big part in the growth of that spirit of camaraderie which became such a unique feature of the 2/5th and which has lasted to this day. He stood watching the Battalion that May morning as the column swung by. It may have been unsoldierly, but it was a spontaneous tribute to the affection in which he was held, that the men of his old Company, though marching to attention, broke into a cheer for its erstwhile leader. And so they marched to War.

It was a hot and dusty road that led to Tidworth Station, for Spring with all her soft green lanes, her leafy shadows, spends none of her allurements on barrack squares and camp roads.

Arrived at the Station the men were herded in a bare yard, beside which stood an equally bare looking troop train. Nothing ever personified the utter lack of human care or sympathy so well as a drill ground, a transport wagon or a troop train. But such things mattered little to those about to realise the goal of all those past weary months of training. They were even grateful for the change of life and surroundings.

Some time about noon the troops were detailed

C

into parties of ten and hustled into stuffy cushionless carriages.

There were a few handshakes, a few messages, a few forced jocularities and then, as the whistle sounded, the train drew slowly out of the station. Some, standing on the platform, smiled through misty eyes, and waved an " au revoir." The band played " Auld Lang Syne ", and hearts ached a little. Those in the densely packed carriages best checked their feelings by sitting back, falling to conversation or indulging in well known military expletives when a rifle butt pressed upon a peevish corn or a water bottle intruded into the region that providence had intended for ribs and for ribs only. Some slept, some ate, a few talked, but the majority merely thought. The old camp at Parkhouse had, after all, been home : it had sheltered them for many a week ; they had crawled back from route marches and field days, footsore and weary and there they had found food and rest ; it was there that they had learned to share in mischance and in pleasures ; the seeds of a real comradeship had germinated on that barren muddy square and in those dingy huts.

The train sped through a panorama of wood and undulating grass land. Familiar scenes brought back many a memory of a dreary foot slogging, followed by an attack in the heat of the day and then a fitful slumber under the lamps of heaven.

In such a frame of mind the hours were dozed away until Southampton was reached. The troops detrained upon a gloomy platform from which they were able to catch their first glimpse of H.M.T. 861, the ship that was destined to bear them away from their native land.

For several hours, it seemed, both officers and men roamed aimlessly about the docks as far as military restrictions would permit, and picked up the latest rumours about raids on the East Coast and torpedoed transport. An enterprising newsboy was shouting " Three German Submarines gone down " and as he pocketed twopence from an unsuspecting patron, he added with a wink, "and they all came up again."

At length the time of embarkation arrived. On going aboard, all ranks were served out with life belts and left to settle down as best they may, while awaiting the hour of departure.

This was announced by the sounding of a syren and the transport moved slowly from the quay. It is impossible to find words to express the thoughts that must have been uppermost in the minds of those men who were leaving England's shores and leaving in her keeping so much that they treasured. Night was just unfolding her wings ; the colours were fading towards the west ; the waves seemed to sigh a little sadly. Till then, few had realised how much was being left behind. Some gazed across the ever increasing stretch of water and watched the receding coastline. The darkness thickened and hid the distant view, but still imagination pictured avenues of beech trees, woods and valleys ; it caught a fragrance of roses and heard voices from home and church bells bidding folks to come. Night grew cold and so, in order to keep warm, the men huddled together about the deck, and their reveries merged into sleep.

Almost before the full realisation of leaving England had matured, the ship reached Havre early on the morning of May 25th. The troops disembarked, formed up and marched through the town, to a temporary camp on the hill. The sight of British soldiers was by this time such a commonplace that no one paid the smallest attention to the Battalion's arrival. As for the Battalion itself, it was much too preoccupied in keeping to the right of the road to take much note of its new environment.

When the camp was reached, the old love of home reasserted itself and the men were soon busy clamouring for field postcards, proud to be able to show their friends that at last they were actually in France and to give them the printed assurance that they had not been admitted to hospital and had received no letters for a long time. At least one man added a postscript " I am in the pink as I hope it finds you." One officer, too, is reputed to have visited an estaminet and to have purchased a bottle of sweet champagne for three and a half francs ; the cork came out with an encouraging " pop " which justified him in writing home to say that he was already within the sound of the guns.

During the time the Battalion remained at this camp, the monotony of life was only relieved by one solitary bathe. Two days later it entrained again and made a twenty-four hours' journey up the line. Few will forget that first experience of a French railway or the language used when, on reaching what was thought to be the destin- ation, it was found that there was yet a seven miles' march to be negotiated before the prospect of a meal.

Eventually a small village called Le Sart was reached and here the Battalion settled into billets for two or three days of comparative rest. As night came on, it was possible to see the glow of the Verey lights in the near distance and to hear the thunder of artillery. Life was becoming frightfully real.

Looking back it had been less than a week since the Battalion had marched away from Salisbury Plain on that serene May morning, but in the intervening time a host of human emotions had been stirred to their depth ; there were the cheers on leaving Parkhouse Camp, the " au revoirs " on the station platform, the silent reveries as the troop- ship slipped from the Quay, the thoughts of home that matured into an intense longing as time went on.

Whatever may be said about the futility of war, it re- awakened human sympathies that had become numbec through disuse ; it brought romance into a complaceni age ; it fused the masses into a common purpose ; through it youth was justified and by it older men were rejuvenated

To have taken part in the war is indeed to have though great thoughts and to have lived till we proved them true

SNIPERS—MAY 1916.

A MACHINE-GUN SECTION.

CHAPTER IV

LAVENTIE DAYS

LE SART had been reached on May 28th. On the following day orders were received for the Battalion to go into the trenches in front of Riez Bailleul for instruction under the London Welsh, then occupying that part of the line.

On May 31st a move was made from Le Sart to Riez Bailleul, a pleasant little hamlet about a mile or so east of La Gorgue. After meeting guides from the London Welsh at this point, the troops moved up to the trenches. That night is one of vivid memories—the curious names of the lanes, Eton Road, Cheltenham Road, Rugby Road—then the main road running from Estaires to La Bassee—then Rouge Croix with its red Crucifix (still standing to this day) and the sentry standing at the cross roads, then, after a long wait the splitting up into small parties and proceeding at intervals along a duckboarded trench—the Verey lights in the near distance, the tat-tat of machine-guns and the occasional whistle of a stray bullet and the instinct to duck. The village of Neuve Chapelle lay on the right.

A further twenty minutes and Sign Post Lane was reached and then the front line breastworks. The night was very dark and the Verey lights from both sides lit up everything at intervals in a ghostly sort of way; there was, too, an uncanny stillness in the air, broken occasionally by some spasmodic firing. It was difficult to imagine that this place had any connection with a world war—it seemed so quiet.

This part of the line was known as the Duck's Bill Sector, on account of the huge crater of that name that lay on the left front and was connected to the front line by a sap. The front line itself was here composed of a high wall of sandbags, with sally ports running out into No Man's Land. The communication trenches, such as Min Street, South and North Tilleloy Streets, were deep and a raised duckboard platform, covered with rabbit wire, made them dry to walk in. These trenches were revetted with hurdles and sometimes with canvas. Battalion Headquarters in this sector was at Ebinezer Farm, about a mile behind the front line. The sector was officially known as the Moated Grange Sector. The week's instruction passed quietly though the Battalion sustained eight casualties. A return to Le Sart was made on June 8th.

On June 10th the Battalion moved forward again to Laventie. Laventie is a place of happy memories to many. It was rather a unique little town, built in the form of a cross, with its red brick church in the centre. Though it was only a mile or so from the front line of the Fauquissart Sector, the civilians lived on there and farmed a certain amount of the land around. The town had suffered considerably in 1915, when it was the scene of fierce house to house fighting, yet the billets were fairly habitable and the plane trees still stood in the streets. There were some beautiful lawns and gardens behind some of the big houses. The nights at Laventie were distinctly noisy, since eighteen pounder batteries, not to mention a fifteen inch railway gun, surrounded the village. But the place itself was seldom shelled : it seemed to be a case of " live and let live." If the Germans shelled Laventie, the British artillery retaliated on Aubers.

While in reserve at Laventie, the Battalion found ration and working parties for the front line and also garrisoned the reserve posts, Fort Esquin, Wangerie and Masselot.

The first independent experience of trench duty in the

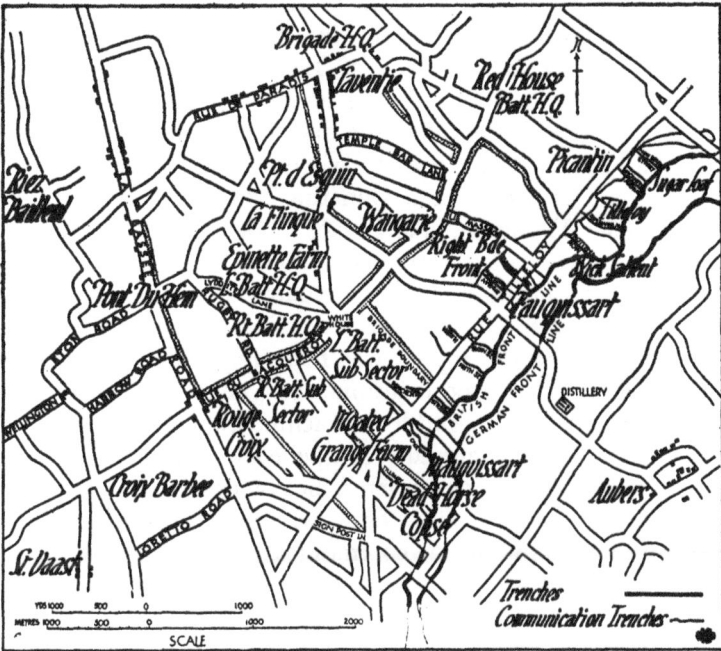

*Laventie, showing
Fauquissart Sector.*

front line was gained when the 2/5th Glosters relieved the 2/1st Bucks on June 15th in the Fauquissart–Laventie Sector. Two events make this tour memorable. One was the lamentable death of Lieut. Clifford Cole of C Company, who was hit by an aerial torpedo. Lieut. Cole was the first officer casualty that the Battalion suffered. He had been with it since its early days and by his efficiency and good nature he had won the esteem of both officers and men. His death, taking place so soon after the Battalion had gone to France, came as a blow. The other event of note was a raid made by A Company under the command of Capt. Wales. Unfortunately, after the raiding party had gone over the top, it was held up by the wire which was found to have been insufficiently cut. The party was thus exposed to a ruthless machine-gun fire from the enemy and was eventually compelled to return to its own trenches after having suffered heavy casualties. For the purpose of the raid, an attempt was made by the signallers to establish lamp signal communication between the front line and Battalion Headquarters, but the difference between a dress rehearsal on a quiet night and the real thing, with Verey lights and gun flashes abounding, had been miscalculated. The signallers on this occasion included Tom Voyce of Twickenham fame. He came to the 2/5th from the 1/5th, having been sent back as being under age. He tells how he was placed in the " awkward " squad. Many who have tried to circumvent Tom Voyce when he was dashing for the goal line in those long loping strides of his, have good reason to know how " awkward " he really was. Many acts of gallantry were performed during the raid and the following awards were made—M.C. to Capt. Wales, D.C.M. to Pte. Fletcher, M.M. to Sgt. Norris and Cpl. Driver. The total casualties were 5 other ranks killed, 1 died of wounds, 3 officers wounded, 13 other ranks wounded and 4 missing. Among the missing was Sgt. Newman of C Company.

It had become an obsession with the Higher Command

to plan all kinds of ruses with the intention of upsetting the morale of the Germans. On one occasion, smoke bombs were hurled out over the parapet and then full-sized cardboard figures, which had previously been laid in No Man's Land, and connected by wires to the front line trenches, were drawn up into a standing position to give the appearance of an attack. At another time sandbags filled with grass were thrown over the top of the breastworks with the same purpose in view. It was never ascertained whether these 'stunts' produced the effect that was intended but they were very unpopular with the men, as they never failed to draw retaliation from the enemy, the full brunt of which fell on the front line troops. Many casualties were suffered in this way and C.Q.M.S. Roberts still preserves a piece of the barrel of his rifle as a memento of one of these pleasant evening amusements.

On June 21st the Battalion was relieved and returned to billets, while on the following day the only notable fact, according to the War Diary, was the death of a pack cob.

On the 27th the Battalion was again in the trenches, where it remained till relieved on July 3rd by the 2/7th Worcesters. It then marched back to billets in La Gorgue.

La Gorgue and Estaires were only separated from each other by a stream. Divisional Headquarters and Divisional Baths, the latter in a large brewery, were situated in La Gorgue. The troops indulged in their first hot bath in France and clothing was disinfected. Estaminets abounded and the inhabitants showed great hospitality and kindness. The British unit that wore the yellow circle is remembered by them to this day.

On July 6th an order was received to move as soon as possible to Richebourg-St. Vaast and to take over from the 4/5th Black Watch. At 5.45 p.m. the Battalion moved from La Gorgue and took over from the Black Watch, and on the 12th it relieved the 2/1st Bucks in the front line of this new sector. Things were pretty lively here, as there had recently been an attack on a salient in the German line. The front line trenches of both sides were very close to one another in places, so close in fact that a bomb could easily be thrown from one to the other, and No Man's Land was littered with the dead bodies of men who had been scythed down by machine-gun fire in the late attack. In this sector were such famous spots as Windy Corner, Chocolate Menier Corner, Factory Post and Port Arthur.

The cemetery at Richebourg was an eerie spot ; it had been completely churned up by shell fire : tombs torn open revealed skeletons that had lain there for years. The crucifix, as was so often the case, remained standing.

On July 15th the Battalion was relieved in this sector, officially known as the Ferme Du Bois Sector, and returned to La Gorgue. It had no sooner arrived and settled into billets here, than it was ordered to move to Estaires, a mile or so away. It was always thought that this order must have emanated from what Ian Hay calls the practical jokes department.

So life went on and tours of trench duty followed by reliefs soon became part of a routine—another instance of the speed with which men get accustomed to new circumstances and new modes of life. The most outstanding example of this faculty is, of course, the way in which men already advanced in the twenties, thirties, and even forties, changed their civilian occupations at a moment's notice and in a comparatively short time, became, if not quite up to the level of the Guards' tradition, tolerably good soldiers and many superlatively good ones. In one respect at least Territorial and other Battalions that had been raised for the war held an advantage over the original Regulars in that they were composed of men from every sort of trade and profession. The 2/5th Glosters, for instance, included in its personnel, members of Parliament, lawyers, bakers, accountants, drapers, musicians, conjurers, butchers, sugar magnates, farm labourers and artisans of every sort. Such a diversity of talent made the social side of life much more entertaining and was probably one of the reasons why actual fighting with all its discomfort and tragedy was faced with such philosophic composure.

Round about the middle of July ominous rumours got about of an impending attack by the 61st Division in co-operation with an Australian Division and movements became irregular. Small groups of Staff Officers and Commanding Officers could be seen, maps in hand, whispering together ; large quantities of artillery began to assemble ; trench mortars commenced to operate more frequently and a " flying pig," memorable because another member of this porcine family had previously registered on this sector, dropped its message short and blown up two or three fire bays on its own side, made its appearance.

These omens materialised when on July 19th an attack was launched. The ostensible objective was the Aubers Ridge, some high ground opposite the British front from which the Germans could command a view of all the movements of their opponents. The real intention of the operation was to keep the German Divisions there so fully occupied that they would not be able to reinforce the troops on the Somme.

The Berks and the Bucks bore the brunt of the attack, while the Oxfords and Glosters were in support and reserve respectively. So far as the Aubers Ridge was concerned the attack failed dismally, but it probably had the effect of keeping the German Divisions there, at any rate, for the time being. The casualties of the 184th Brigade were very heavy, the Bucks being especially hard hit. The lot that fell to the Glosters was the depressing task of bringing in and burying the dead. This operation took three or four days to complete and it is notable that the Germans allowed the stretcher-bearers and others to wander about No Man's Land in broad daylight, picking up the dead and wounded, without firing a shot.

Writing of the Aubers Ridge calls to mind an amusing

episode. It was a standing order that men in the front line should occasionally fire a round or two over the ridge. The idea was that stray bullets dropping into the village of Aubers would have a demoralising effect. As the distance was considerable, this entailed firing at a high trajectory and with open sights. It was no uncommon sight to find a man kneeling on the fire step with his rifle resting on the top of the breastwork at an angle of 45° and complacently loosing off a round—but there is no record that any such bullet ever found a billet in Aubers. On one occasion the Germans shelled the front line rather heavily and a suspicious looking haze began to emanate from their front line ; Klaxon horns were sounded, trenches were manned and an order was given to open rapid fire on the enemy's front line. An officer going round discovered a Tommy crouching in a fire bay and with his rifle canted at an angle of about 60° letting off round after round into the air as fast as he could. " And what the —— are you firing at ? " bellowed the officer. " Six hundred," replied the man. Such is the force of habit.

The night of July 27th/28th was an exciting one for the Battalion, as the Germans took it into their heads to make a surprise attack on the Duck's Bill Crater.

Normally the Duck's Bill Crater was unoccupied except for a small sentry group or two. As the crater was in A Company's sector, the duty of providing these sentries fell to that Company. At about 10 p.m. the Germans opened a heavy bombardment on the front line with the idea, it is presumed, of preventing support from reaching the crater before they had occupied it and made good their position. Capt. Rickerby, however, who was commanding A Company, acted with admirable decision and foresight. As soon as the bombardment started he moved most of his men from the front line along the sap and into the crater, in order to avoid casualties from the shell fire. The consequence was that when the Germans arrived to take possession of what they expected to be a practically un-

DUCK'S BILL CRATER, LAVENTIE FRONT.

occupied crater, they found to their surprise a large body of troops ready to receive them. So far, therefore, as a frontal attack was concerned they were checkmated. Sgt. Webb, however, realised the possibility of the enemy working round and taking the crater in the rear. He, therefore, formed a strong bombing group under his own command in the sap at point *b* in the sketch. Thus he had only a small front to defend and was in a position to repel any attack that may be made by way of the sap. After several vain efforts to make headway and after suffering several casualties, the raiders retired. They were not, however, done with and at 11.20 p.m. another attack was launched, but again the defence was ready, for Capt. Rickerby, surmising the possibility of a further visit, had not withdrawn his men. This time the Germans brought a machine-gun with them which was placed on the further lip of the crater. The effect of this gun was, however, neutralised by L/Cpl. Davies, who had in the interim brought up his Lewis gun section and taken up a position at *a*. The German gun was very quickly put out of action and the Lewis gun did great execution on the advancing raiders. As a final effort an attempt was made on the sap. Two or three men actually got into the trench, but they were immediately put out of action by the bombing group. One of the men captured during this operation was found to have in his possession a complete telephone apparatus, which seemed to point to the fact that the Germans had intended to occupy the crater permanently.

From the Battalion's point of view and from A Company's in particular, the episode was a brilliant piece of work. Capt. Rickerby and Lieut. Varcoe were both awarded the M.C., while Sgt. Webb and L/Cpl. Davies gained the D.C.M., and Ptes. Humphries, Davies, Hester, Mundy, Sanders and Smith gained the M.M.

No awards were more deservedly won.

It is permissible after a lapse of fourteen years to divulge one of the secrets of the War. It concerns the withdrawal of an Australian mining section from the Duck's Bill Sector because of indications that the Germans were about to blow a mine beneath the crater. The indications were caused by two lads of C Company, 2/5th Glosters, who were acting as a sentry post in the crater. There was a considerable amount of water in the crater and these two enterprising youths, in order to test its depth, amused themselves by tossing into it a series of Mills bombs. The depth of the water proved to be such that comparatively little disturbance was caused on its surface by the explosions, but the earth shook violently and the full force of the detonations reached the Australians who were complacently sapping in the bowels of Mother Earth. Scared men rushed into the crater to ascertain from the watchful sentries if they had heard or seen anything, but sometimes it is policy for sentries to " lie still." On this occasion, they did so ; they had seen or heard nothing. The result was the withdrawal of all miners from the area owing to hostile mining activities.

One of the strong points of the British soldier was his inability to take war seriously, but whereas many writers paint him as taking his amusements in philandering, drinking and singing lewd songs, this episode shows that his irresponsibilities generally took the form of harmless devilment, that most priceless quality in human nature.

LT.-COL. P. BALFOUR, D.S.O.
Commanding Officer, March 1916—April 1917.

.

CHAPTER V

LAVENTIE DAYS—(continued)

AUGUST 1916 opened with the Battalion in billets at La Gorgue. The usual routine of movement followed all too quickly, for on the 9th it moved to Laventie to garrison the posts Wangerie, Masselot and Fort Esquin, D Company taking over part of the front line from the 2/7th Worcesters.

About this time Lieut. Worsley was wounded while on patrol, and 2nd Lieut. F. W. Harvey was reported missing, but happily he lived to write the story of his captivity.

During this tour of duty C Company made a raid on the night 19th/20th August.

The rough outline of the trenches that were raided was an inverted T, a front line stretch of some eighty yards with a communication trench running back from the centre.

The raiding party was divided into six sections : two were to act as flank guard ; a third was to be the covering party, and was detailed to take up its position on the parapet of the German front line trench ; the other three parties were to enter the German trench at the same point and to work respectively right, left and up the communication trench. The signal for the attack was to be the first shot from the artillery which, it had been arranged, would open fire on the enemy's support line and shorten to the front line immediately after the raiders had evacuated the trenches.

Two novelties were introduced into the plan. Firstly, the raid was to be made on the same night and an hour or so after a similar operation had been carried out on exactly the same sector by another battalion. Secondly, the preliminary bombardment was to be dispensed with.

47

In these ways it was hoped to take the enemy by surprise—and this indeed proved to be the case.

So much then for the general plan, in case other ardent souls may care to indulge in this specialised form of recreation should another war occur.

In preparation for the raid the Company spent the previous fortnight behind the lines. Each day the attack was rehearsed on some disused trenches which approximately resembled the plan of those to be raided. Each night No Man's Land was carefully reconnoitred.

The remainder of the days and nights were eked out in eating, smoking, singing, sleeping, cleaning equipment and other amusements which are supposed to foster morale. Despite the hope unuttered that the war might end on August 18th, the fateful day rolled round. The raiders trudged up to the front line about 10 p.m. and spent a desultory hour or so quaffing rum and blackening hands and faces. At about 12.45 a.m. they moved out into No Man's Land, and the various sections took up their allotted positions, the three that were to enter the trenches, and the covering party, lying down in a ditch which ran nearly parallel to the German line and about forty yards from it. All right up till now—as the American said as, after having fallen from the roof of a skyscraper, he passed the ninth story window.

Everything was depressingly quiet, as is usually the case just before a raid. A light mist hanging over the scene lent an eeriness to the picture : an occasional Verey light alone relieved the darkness ; nothing was so audible as one's breathing ; the merest whisper jarred.

Thus they waited. Some dozed nonchalantly ; some watched the luminous hand moving slowly yet inexorably towards the hour of zero. One minute still to go—thirty seconds—fifteen—ten ! There was a slight bracing of limbs. Suddenly—a sound from far behind—faint, but unmistakable—the guns had opened fire. The raiders rose up and, rushing towards the German trenches, reached

48

CAPT. A. F. BARNES, M.C.
(*Editor*).
Officer Commanding C Company.

MAJOR THE RIGHT HON.
C. P. ALLEN.
Officer Commanding C Company.

them as the first shell burst on the support line. What, a moment ago, might have been a meadow outlying some English village, was now a cauldron of flame and metal. The night air was riven by screaming shells; hundreds of Verey lights transmuted the darkness into a dazzling carnival; the quivering gun flashes from the German counter-barrage illumined the distant sky-line; the rat-tat-tat of innumerable Vickers guns, the muffled explosion of bombs; the ear-piercing bursts of the 4.9's completed the transformation. The enemy was taken completely by surprise, as is shown by the fact that the first sentry whom the raiders encountered was still looking out over No Man's Land and was bayonetted through the back. Dugouts were bombed as well as several of the enemy who were endeavouring to escape.

The battle was at its height when a shell from one of our batteries, falling short, burst in the fire bay close to one of the raiding sections. A certain amount of disorganisation resulted and, taking advantage of the occasion, some cute German shouted "Retire." The raiders, taking the order to be a genuine one, immediately scrambled out of the German lines. The guns almost at the same time shortened their range on to the enemy's front line, so that the mistake was of little consequence.

It had been prearranged that the sections should re-assemble in the ditch from which the attack started, the flankers naturally remaining where they were. This was done in order that the party on returning might not get caught by the German barrage which was then falling heavily on the Battalion's front line. Only one member of the entire party disregarded the precaution and unfortunately was killed just before he reached the safety of his own trenches. The rest remained out in No Man's Land for forty or fifty minutes while the shells from both sides hissed and shrieked overhead. Eventually the British Artillery barrage died down and ceased and the German guns followed suit in a few minutes. When all was quiet

D

again, the party walked back to its trenches without sustaining a single casualty on the journey.

The Company's losses were one officer, Lieut. Jackson, killed and eleven other ranks wounded. The enemy must have suffered much more severely.

The raid was over. As though a reproving voice had spoken, the powers of destruction had faded out, that Nature's more placid requiem might harbinger the dawn.

Those who had taken part in the night's adventure ambled back to billets and slept dreamlessly.

It would be invidious to name individuals among the raiders when all played their several parts so well. Everyone was animated by loyalty both to the Company and to his comrades and in this none failed. Those who came through unscathed were happy to be alive. Yes, but trench raids were becoming a habit. More happy were those who, though wounded, would soon see the white cliffs of Dover looming through the mist. Happiest of all, perhaps, was he who had seemed to pass so easily, so painlessly into the unexplored—"felix mortis occasione."

Nothing of any further importance so far as active operations are concerned occurred on the Laventie Front, though the Battalion remained there till October 27th when it moved to Robecq and thence, southward, to take part in the campaign on the Somme.

Capt. J. Hollington, who had been in command of D Company since its early days, was evacuated sick in September. Capt. Barnes was accidentally wounded on a course early in October, and about the same time Capt. G. F. Davies, B Company's commander, was attached to 61st Divisional School as Instructor. Such changes, together with the casualties in killed and wounded, which had mounted almost daily since the Battalion had been in France, altered the complexion of its personnel considerably. While new drafts brought many strange faces, many familiar ones were missed. Nevertheless, judged in the light of later

CAPT. J. E. HOLLINGTON.
Officer Commanding D Company.

MAJOR G. F. DAVIES, M.P.
Officer Commanding B Company.

experiences, the Laventie front was a peaceful spot and everyone was sorry to leave it. Certainly, there were unpleasant moments when, as Pte. George Winfield says, the principal amusement consisted in running along badly fitting duckboards and dodging " minnies." Then there was the dank smell of sodden sandbags and the rats. Yes, but there were also the poppies in No Man's Land and the roses trailing up the walls of the ruined cottages—Nature's compensations for the wantonness of man.

The man in the trenches always considered the raid as an overrated pursuit ; it was supposed to have a demoralising effect on the enemy, but this no one was ever able to prove ; that it had a stimulating effect on those that carried it out is extremely doubtful, whatever may be said about fostering the fighting spirit.

Patrolling No Man's Land, uncanny and perilous as it often was, was one of the least unpleasant of trench duties— at worst it afforded a sense of release from the constricted conditions of a front line trench ; there must have been many who would have done two patrols rather than once have to put up wire or carry gas cylinders up the line. Some of the essential duties of officers were often exasperating and not infrequently unpleasant. In the former class no one who has been through it will ever forget the Returns which were being constantly demanded by Brigade and Battalion Headquarters. Who does not remember the typed order, " Companies will render to H.Q. by 12.00 the number of petrol tins taken over by them." If it was not petrol tins it was pots of plum and apple. And then, when Headquarters grew specially impatient, a second order, " Expedite rendition of return, please," whatever language that idiom belongs to.

Among the more unpleasant duties of officers was the censoring of letters, for no one with a sense of decency wants to read other persons' private correspondence. " The boys are all well and we have just taken cascara," one man wrote. The officer crossed out the word " cascara," explaining to the man that names of places must not be mentioned.

However, it requires but a grain of true philosophy and even some of the horrors of war become mere inconveniences. It became a commonplace to see a man sitting on a fire step on a quiet sunny morning, with his shirt off, running his fingers along the seams and humming complacently to himself that memorable ditty, " I'm so chatty." In army slang the process was known as " reading a shirt." The purists will curl their lips over this, while wiser men know it to be a part of a new sangfroid that enabled men to face discomfort with equanimity.

CHAPTER VI

ON THE SOMME

ARRIVING at Robecq on October 27th, 1916, the Battalion trekked southward in stages until it reached Albert, with its famous leaning virgin, on November 20th. It was on this date that Capt. G. L. Day, Hunts Cyclists, reported for duty.

It was a tremendous business to procure billets in ruined Albert and everything was vastly different from the area that had just been left. Here was war with a vengeance ! The whole place was packed with troops and transport, and the traffic along the Albert–Bapaume road was incessant—guns, limbers, lorries, men, mules and ambulances.

During the only night the Battalion remained in Albert rain fell continuously. Company commanders rode forward to reconnoitre the line and on the following day the troops were moved up to occupy trenches in front of Grandecourt. The contrast between the sectors in front of Laventie and the Somme crater fields was striking. Here were primitive conditions—men clinging to shell holes, mud deep enough to completely submerge a gun team and limber, masses of unburied dead strewn over the battle fields ; no sign of organised trenches, but merely shell holes joined up to one another—and, last, but by no means least in importance, no landmarks anywhere. The whole scene was one bleak wilderness of death.

Capt. Sinclair gives a graphic account of reconnoitring this part of the line.

53

" From Mouquet Farm guides took each of us to our appointed sectors. I shall never forget this day as long as I live. My guide took me on to the tramway which ran from Tullock's Corner to Rifle Dump in Zollern Trench. There was a white November fog and a pretty thick one at that. When we got to Rifle Dump we left the tramway and ploughed across the open. We had started from Albert at about midday and it was now 3 p.m. We got hopelessly lost. I have dim recollections of shell fire, of fog, of dead bodies, of Hessian Trench and of eventually striking that cheerful spot appropriately named Death Valley. The guide had completely lost his bearings. He left me on a duckboard track somewhere near Hessian Trench, promising to return after finding out where he was. He was away about an hour and a half and when he did return, it was getting dark. Somehow or other we struggled on through the mud, stumbled over dead bodies and floundered into water-logged shell holes, till we luckily struck the Ravine. It was now about 7 p.m. Three hours later we set out on the long trail back to Albert, which, thanks to a ' lorry jump ' from Pozieres, we eventually reached more dead than alive in the early hours of the morning. The average rate of progression over that crater field could not, at the most, have been more than a mile in two hours. Then came the job of leading the various companies to their sectors. We started off at 2 p.m. on the 21st and met our guides at Tullock's Corner. We were shelled the whole way up to our positions and the relief was not completed till 2 a.m. on the 22nd, the code word for ' relief complete ' being ' another little drink won't do us any harm '— another invention of the Practical Jokes Department.

" In the front line the mud made movement of any sort practically impossible until the frost hardened the ground ; shaving was not to be thought of ; ration parties were held up in the mire and so we were down to one cup of cold tea per man per day, hence the aptness of the above code word. The shelling was so incessant that we were

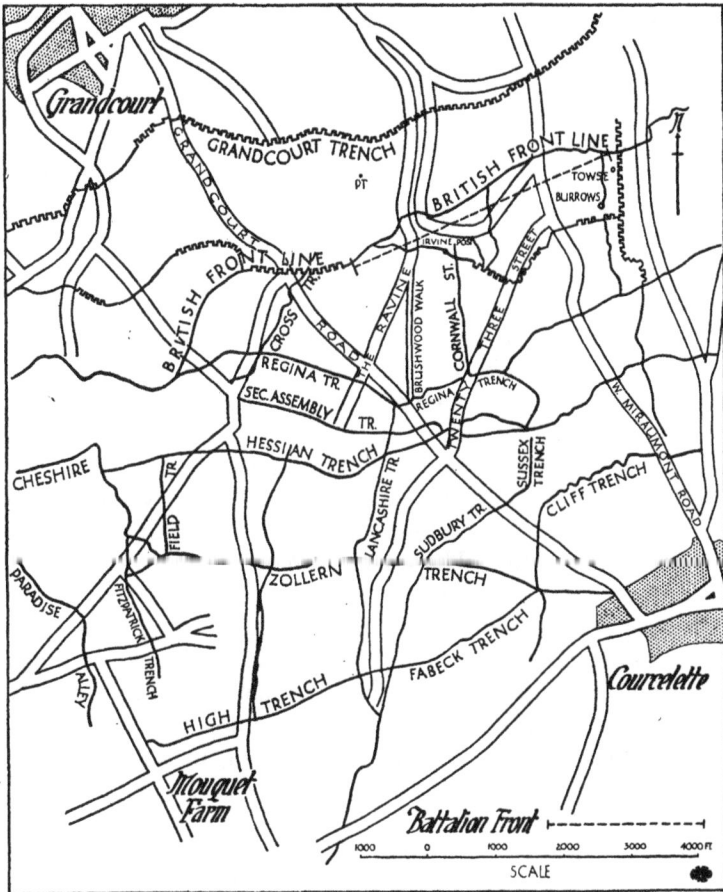

The Trench System in front of Grandecourt.

THE STORY OF THE

compelled to live more like rats than men. After three or four days of this existence, we were relieved on November 26th and marched back to Wellington Huts."

The Battalion was back in the trenches again in the forward zone on December 20th, but was again relieved on the 24th and on the 30th it moved to Varennes and remained out of the line for a month, spent largely in training at Gapennes.

When talking of an Infantry Battalion, one is apt to think only of the man with a rifle who actually fights as an individual. There are, however, many other essential services in an infantry unit upon which the efficiency of the rifleman depends. Among these none is more important than the signal service. The duty of the signaller is to keep communication intact under all circumstances, and to do this he is often called upon to face the gravest risks. Sgt. Child well illustrates the importance of the signaller's duties and the dangers he faces in accomplishing them.

" The scene," he writes, " is Headquarters Signal Office in Zollern trench. The operator receives a report from A Company, who are holding the front line, of heavy enemy shelling ; he communicates the message to the C.O. who asks to be put through to the Company ; the operator plugs in, but gets no reply. The line has been broken. A corporal and a linesman prepare to go along to A Company's line ; they dash up the steps of the dugout and dive into the trench to wallow knee deep in slush. After plunging along for fifty yards, the linesman taps in and calling Battalion, is answered immediately : the break is further afield—they must go on. Presently the line disappears over the top and they follow it out into the open ground where their only shelter from continuous gun fire is waterlogged shell holes. They scramble on, holding the telephone line for guidance until ahead of them they can dimly see the white outline of Regina trench. There is the screaming sound of a shell and they drop into the nearest shell hole just as, with a blinding flash, the earth ten yards ahead is churned up ; they rush into the trench, tap in

MEMORIES OF ABLAINCOURT. 1917.

again and again are answered by Battalion, but still there is no reply from A Company. On they must go again, out into the open and into Death Valley over which a barrage is raging—evidently this is where the line is broken. Ultimately after much stumbling, searching and a few comments on shells and Germans in general, one broken end is found and then the other, some forty or fifty yards away. The two men now crouch in a pot hole and join the ends ; a phone, which the linesman always carries with him, is connected and at last A Company is spoken to. It looks as though their task is now done, but alas ! it is now found that no reply is forthcoming from Battalion—another breakage—two more loose ends to be found and repaired —more comments on shells and Germans. All the above experiences have to be gone through again till finally complete communication is restored and the signallers return to the shelter of their dugout, worn out but proud in the knowledge that their duty has been well and bravely done.''

From Gapennes the Battalion marched on February 7th, 1917, to L'Etoile. Thence it proceeded further south by train, arriving at Wiencourt, some fifteen miles east-south-east of Amiens on the 13th. It moved to Framerville two days later, and on the 16th relieved the 2nd Battalion 101st French Infantry Regiment in the Ablaincourt Sector. Since the offensive had died down, this sector had been very quiet, but seemingly for the special benefit of the 184th Brigade, the Germans now brought up their travelling circus, as it was called. There was a considerable amount of gas shelling here and the activity culminated in a raid being made on the Oxfords on February 28th. The preliminary barrage over the whole sector was so heavy that Capt. Badcock, who was on the right of the Oxfords, naturally concluded that a general assault was imminent. He, therefore, proceeded to discharge S.O.S. rockets from the bottom of his dugout steps. As the rockets were gaily discharged, he was discomfited by hearing a savage yell and much bad language. It transpired that a plump company cook had taken shelter from the bombardment at the top of the dugout steps and was a little upset at being bombarded in the rear by his own Company Commander—another of the " stern " realities of war !

During this period, " trench foot " became a very serious problem, and a very large number of men had to be evacuated because of its effects.

The Battalion moved into Brigade Reserve at Raincourt on March 9th. Billets in this village, though the buildings were in ruins, provided a certain amount of comfort and were a distinct relief from the truly horrible conditions on the front line. For the most part, when in Reserve on the Somme front, the men had to exist in conditions nearly as bad as those in the forward zone. The shelling, too, was very heavy at this time in the back areas, presumably because the enemy was shooting off some of his surplus stock of ammunition, preparatory to his withdrawal to the Hindenburg Line. At any rate, he made it increasingly difficult to move about and what trenches there were became so impossible that when it was necessary to move from one point to another, both officers and men preferred to risk the open ground even in broad daylight.

March 17th was a day of tremendous excitement and there were animated flutterings in the dovecots of the Higher Command. The Germans were retiring.

The Battalion was actually at Guillancourt when the news of the German retirement became definitely known. The men had been hoping for a well-earned rest, but instead they received orders to be ready to move forward at an hour's notice. The move took place the following morning, March 18th, but the Battalion made the journey without some of its officers, who were at the time indulging in Amiens leave.

Vermandovillers was reached at 1.15 p.m., and the troops became road menders for the next ten days.

The Germans had done things very thoroughly : villages were devastated, all fruit trees cut down, all cross-roads

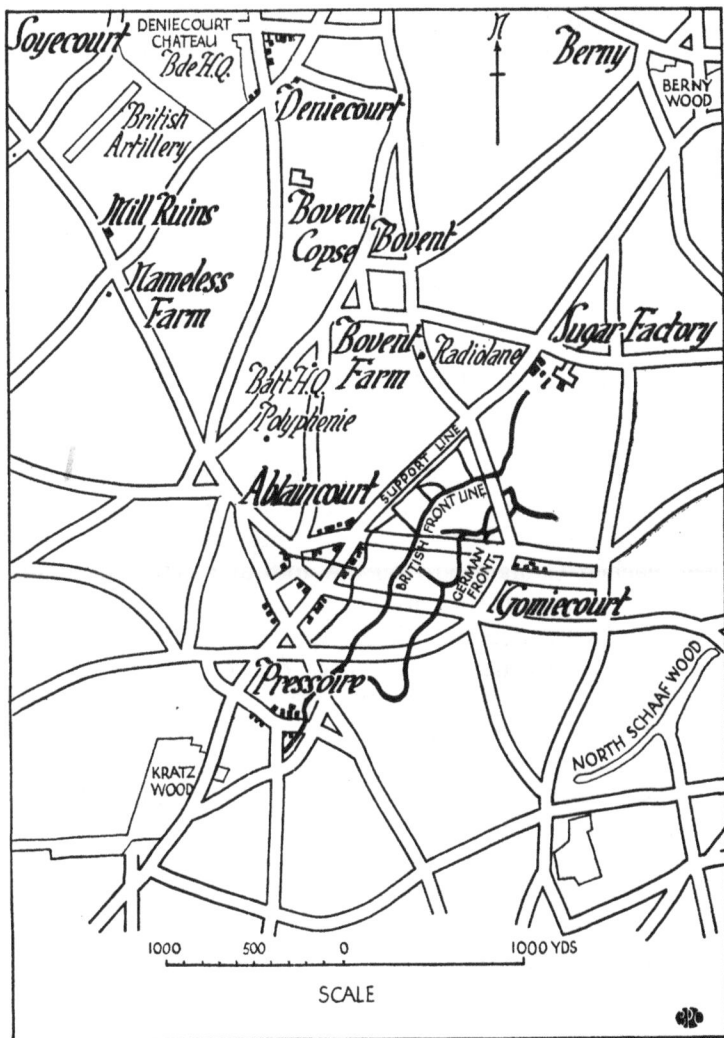

The Ablaincourt Sector.

mined, all wells rendered useless. Knowing that the allies would follow them in their withdrawal, the enemy had made the pursuit as difficult as possible. It reminded one of the man who, because his loving spouse had expressed her intention of dancing on his grave, left instructions with his executors to bury him at sea.

" We followed them," Capt. Sinclair writes, " slowly and suspiciously over a vast tract of wilderness, but we were glad of the respite from mud, shells and the cramped conditions of trench warfare. We stopped for five days at Omiecourt working on the roads to enable our guns and transport to go forward. At this time we dug defensive posts west of the Somme at Epenancourt. Slowly we moved on. By night the horizon was illumined by the glare of burning villages and there were frequent sounds of exploding ammunition dumps. The German retirement, carefully planned and as methodically carried out, was in full swing along the whole front. After passing Croix Moligneaux we reached Caulaincourt on the 30th at 5 p.m. Caulaincourt is memorable for its magnificent chateau (in ruins) and for its mausoleum. The latter was the one building we came across that had not been destroyed. Two of the companies decided to risk all traps in the shape of mines and to sleep there. Prophets of ill omen protested on the folly of such an enterprise and predicted all kinds of horrible deaths. However, the mausoleum still stands, though on that occasion it proved to be a precious uncomfortable dormitory and to have obtained any sleep on its draughty stone floor would have been an achievement beyond the powers even of the 2/5th Glosters. On the last day of March patrols were sent forward to ascertain if the village of Vermand had been evacuated. This was found to be the case and A Company was sent up to consolidate east of the village. Whilst digging we saw Uhlans skirmishing in Holnon Wood—they made off towards Bihecourt, about a mile east of Vermand and our rifle fire had no effect on them. This was the first and only time that I saw German

Cavalry in the War. An A Company patrol was sent out on the night of March 31st/April 1st to discover if Bihecourt was still occupied by the enemy. It was a bright moonlight night and we set off under cover of the trees which lined the banks of the Omignon river. On our left front, standing on the road, was a tall isolated poplar tree. When we got near to this tree, we could see an enemy machine-gun post silhouetted against the sky line. We lay "doggo" for ten minutes and listened, then someone sneezed and we were spotted. We got back at the double, having quite decided that Bihecourt was occupied."

On the morning of April 2nd the village of Bihecourt was attacked. A Company took the main part in the attack. In co-operation with an 18-Pdr. Battery, the attackers started forward from the railway embankment north-east of Vermand and three-quarters of a mile from Bihecourt. Very few casualties were suffered, though 2nd Lieut. Durand, in charge of the first wave, was hit through keeping too close to the barrage. A machine-gun which opened fire on the approaching troops was captured together with a few prisoners. As the Germans were found, some shaving and some having breakfast, they had clearly been taken by surprise, and so resistance was easily overcome. After capturing the village, A Company pushed through the village and dug in in an orchard on the east side.

Lieut. (afterwards Capt.) Sinclair was awarded the M.C. for his courageous work on this occasion.

On April 7th B and C Companies made a further attack on the enemy's rearguard positions. Lieut. Pakeman and Sgt. Davis figure in the war diary as having done distinguished service. It was, however, a costly operation as the Battalion lost 7 officers wounded, 15 other ranks killed, and 27 other ranks wounded.

Easter Day, the 8th, was spent in rest at Vermand.

After a period of training in delightful spring weather at Tetry, Canizy and Germaine, the Battalion moved forward to the Fayet front, two miles north-west of St. Quentin.

No one will ever forget the belfry of St. Quentin's Cathedral, which overlooked every movement that took place in the British lines, or the coloured lights that went up continuously every night from it, like roman candles on a Bank Holiday.

While in the neighbourhood of Germaine, C.Q.M.S. Roberts was in charge of the Sergeants' Mess, and he had to ride into Nesle for supplies, a proceeding that was contrary to orders unless supported by an officer's signature. Roberts —like every good quartermaster sergeant—cultivated an elastic conscience, wrote the words " C.Q.M.S. Roberts has permission, et cetera," and blandly signed a fictitious officer's signature. Truly in war necessity knows no laws.

The Fayet Sector consisted of a series of isolated posts ; it was, in fact, an outpost line. All the roads leading up to the village were constantly shelled and the village itself was no health resort. In rear and running parallel to the front held by the Glosters was the famous sunken road and on the bank of the road stood the " Monument," an obelisk erected as a memorial to some troops that took part in the Franco-Prussian War.

The Battalion was now so depleted in numbers that it was reorganised on a three Company basis, with three platoons to a Company.

Behind this front, about a mile from Fayet, lay the village of Holnon, with its two Crucifixes at the Cross-Roads. Holnon was frequently shelled and from the front line the red brick dust could be seen flying into the air as each shell burst in the village.

Work in this sector consisted mainly in strengthening the outpost line, wiring by night and generally consolidating the position. It was good to be on virgin soil, hitherto untouched by war, though most of the villages such as Holnon, Savy and Salency, had been ruthlessly destroyed by the enemy. At first there were no communication trenches, movement had to be made across the open, and a good deal of ingenuity was needed in order to keep on the reverse slopes and so avoid the malignant eye of the Cathedral belfry which appeared never to cease its vigil.

LT.-COL. G. F. COLLETT, D.S.O.
Commanding Officer, April 1917—March 1918.

CHAPTER VII

IN FRONT OF ST. QUENTIN

IT was at this time, on April 20th, 1917, that Major G. F. Collett, late commanding 1/5th Glosters, reported for duty. This officer joined the Battalion at Beauvois just before the Battalion moved up to the front line trenches. It had no knowledge of his arrival, so he was delivered over into the safe keeping of the Q.M. (Lieut. Gledhill) and the Transport Officers (Lieuts. Bright and Davis), who made life very comfortable for him.

His first impression of the Battalion was that it was very tired after its long spell on the Somme Front during the winter.

D Company had been scrapped and the remaining three Companies were weak. But behind this weakness there was a stern determination to carry on at all costs, a spirit that was characteristic of the Battalion and preserved right to the end of its service.

While the Brigadier was on leave, Col. Balfour took command of the Brigade and Major Collett temporarily commanded the Battalion.

About this time Maj.-Gen. Sir Ivor Maxse was building his Corps Line, or third line of defence. Tasks were set on this line and when finished the units engaged could march for home. This scheme produced digging of a very high order and one platoon finished its task, which was intended to take two hours, in thirty-five minutes. An enterprising young Staff Officer happened to spot this, so that tasks were doubled, then trebled, with the result that the rate of work slowed down perceptibly. A willing horse must not be driven too hard.

On May 13th the Battalion moved out of the line, first to Nesle and then by train to Cagny.

Some impressions of the thoroughness of the German retreat from the Somme to the St. Quentin Front will not be out of place. It was thorough, brutally thorough. They had devastated the evacuated area ; blown up houses and blown down garden walls ; they had cut down every tree that could afford shelter to troops or guns ; they had exploded great craters at every cross-roads ; and they had placed delayed mines in nearly every cellar.

All this is undoubtedly war ; but it is one thing to be thorough and quite another thing to be merely foolish ; for to go to the extent of hacking down even the rose bushes in cottage gardens could not possibly have had any justification. Marching out of this area no one could fail to be struck by the piteous sight of fruit trees lying on their sides in full bloom and leaf, which, in a few days, could only wither and decay. War is not a kid glove affair, and after all, other great war captains had done the same thing in the past, notably Hannibal in Italy, and Sherman " as he marched towards the sea."

On May 15th the Battalion went into huts at Cagny. Lieut. Frank Wooster, sent forward on billetting duty, a gay and cheery officer, struck a non-stop lorry and got to Amiens, and when the Battalion arrived the acting C.O. had to billet the officers. Hearing that billets were procurable in the annexe of the Nunnery, he went to interview the Mother Superior and unwittingly made his way into the main building where no male had trod for at least a hundred years. He was, however, forgiven and the billets were good. Lieut. Wooster arrived later from Amiens, pleased with life, somewhat jaded, but very apologetic.

Two days later the Battalion moved to good billets at Monton Villers. All will remember this place because previous troops had shot a mother boar in the woods and her two children, pretty little animals, were being looked after by a farmer. It was also here that the Battalion started practising the new methods of attack ; to many, these appeared too stereotyped and tended to diminish individual action and initiative ; no doubt they were sound, but they were inelastic.

The days following were engaged in marching to the Arras Front. The great offensive here, pushed beyond its legitimate limits, was practically over, so the Battalion could only claim to be in it as clearing-up troops.

All night the enemy would shell Arras with long-range high velocity shells. These generally pitched in the Station Square, a most unhealthy spot. Air raids on Arras were of almost nightly occurrence, and the Brigade Transport suffered very heavily one night when a bomb pitched on the stables. By day Arras was a jolly place : there were several Pierrot troups, including the Divisional Follies under Lieut. Hawkins of the Warwicks, and the Brigade Bands used to play in the Grand Place in the evenings.

Col. Balfour arrived back on May 25th, as Brig.-Gen. the Hon. Robert White had returned from leave. The Brigadier was a man of astounding energy—cool and brave, and knowing what he wanted of his battalions, determined to get it, and thus he made his Brigade, the 184th, one of the best fighting units in France.

For a week the Battalion practised trench attacks on the old German front line system at Wailly, which lies south-west of Arras. The strength of these trenches was amazing—no wonder it cost so much to smash through them. Particularly interesting were the tunnelled machine-gun emplacements, often well in front of their wire.

While at Wailly a tank demonstration was witnessed. On June 1st the Battalion took over trenches in front of Guemappe and was in the line for several days, the principal work consisting of wiring and consolidating.

On these wiring expeditions it was a sorry sight to see so many unburied dead, principally Scotch, lying about.

65   E

Many were buried decently by the Battalion. One field officer was picked up and the Army was anxious to know if it was the body of " The Macintosh " that had been missing for some time, but no identification could be found.

On June 8th Col. Balfour was awarded a well-merited D.S.O. He was given leave and Major Collett again took over command.

The Battalion was relieved and eventually moved to Bernaville, where training took place. The Brigadier, after watching the Battalion carry out a trench attack, was dissatisfied and ordered another. The Fates were against him, for just as the second attack started a thunderstorm broke. The Brigadier had no coat and so, like the men, he got soaked to the skin ; but even this did not damp his enthusiasm. The Battalion got its reward in an ample supply of rum, borrowed from the Bucks Quartermaster, as its own stock of that excellent commodity had run dry.

On June 23rd a move was made to Buire-au-Bois, and Col. Balfour returned from leave. Buire-au-Bois was a lovely village, full of pretty little farmsteads and strawberry gardens. The move there was made for the purpose of rest, reorganisation and training, but of the first very little was experienced.

Col. Balfour left the Battalion on the 29th to take up the duties of Commandant of the 3rd Army Musketry School. By his departure the Battalion realised that it had not only lost a capable and gallant Commanding Officer, but also a very great friend. He will always be remembered as the man who made the Battalion in war. Major Collett was appointed to succeed Col. Balfour in command.

Before leaving, Col. Balfour had elaborated a scheme of training based on Platoon Competitions. Major Collett set to work to get it going, and it proved an enormous success, so successful in fact that the Division circulated the scheme among the other units and instructed them to follow suit.

In these competitions it was interesting to note how many of the young Platoon Officers, soaked in trench warfare,

WARRANT OFFICERS AND SERGEANTS AT BUIRE-AU-BOIS—JULY 1917.

(In centre, R.S.M. W. W. Spragg and R.Q.M.S. A. R. N. Joseland.)

behaved when set a simple exercise in open warfare. Many advanced from a wood in trench formation at the high port. However, you learn quickly by making mistakes, and the enemy machine-gun was only a log of wood, so no damage was done. One competition was " turn out," and it was noteworthy how well C.S.M. Allaway's party always turned out. This Warrant Officer was not asked to turn out his own kit, but the Commanding Officer had few doubts that he had faked his pack to give it that perfectly rectangular look.

More training followed and then the Brigade Horse Show. Major Collett had promised the Transport that if they pooled the prize money, he would double it. Though possessing indifferent cattle, they managed to pull off 1st and 3rd limbers, 3rd travelling kitchens, 1st mules and 2nd officer's charger. Their successes were largely due to the keenness of Lieuts. Bright and Davis, and to their transport rank and file. The Brigadier won the 1st officer's charger from Major Collett on quality, but this was not surprising as a Colonel could hardly ever get a new charger from the Base other than a cab horse that was drawing the old age pension.

During this period Lieut. Wooster asked to be allowed to form a Battalion Concert Party, which he christened the " Cheeryohs." It was a great success and was a valuable means of amusing the men during the evenings in rest. A short account of the " Cheeryohs " is given in a subsequent chapter.

On July 7th sports, organised by R.S.M. Spragg, were held. The tit-bit was the Officers' mule race. It was started with the Band in its rear. The new Commanding Officer kept his seat with becoming dignity, but he was very much an " also ran " as his diminutive mount was not bred as a weight carrier or stayer !

During this time many reinforcements arrived and it was therefore necessary to re-form D Company, disbanded in the winter months. The Commanding Officer decided to select the company himself and asked the Company Commanders to abide loyally by his decisions. The new Company soon settled down with good team work under the energetic and efficient command of Capt. Seymour Tubbs, assisted by his second in command, Capt. Leonard Dudbridge.

The Commanders of the four Companies, A, B, C, D, were now respectively Capt. Rickerby, Major Day, Capt. Badcock and Capt. Tubbs. Later in the war all were killed except Major Day, and the highest memories of their prowess and charm will abide always. Major Gilbert Beloe became second in command of the Battalion, and Capt. H. V. Gray was appointed as Adjutant. Both these officers were splendid organisers and the Battalion wheels were thus always well oiled. Mention must also be made of the Medical Officer, Capt. Lander, whose cheery whistle, enthusiasm for chess, entire disregard of the enemy, and other little foibles, were always inspiring.

After a few days of final polish, Buire-au-Bois, that lovely haven of rest, was left and the Battalion moved nearer to the Ypres Front to take its part in the great offensive which was impending.

A short description of the conditions under which the third Battle of Ypres was fought is here necessary.

The ruined town of Ypres was the centre of what is known as the Salient, which was lightly held by British troops. Eastward, beyond the British line, lay a vast low-lying and slightly undulating plain running down to the sluggish and dirty River Steenbeeke. Beyond this stream the plain rose slowly till it culminated in the famous Passchendaele Ridge. Behind this ridge, which was the objective of the attack, sat the German gunners with perfect observation over the plain right up to and beyond Ypres. The Germans with characteristic thoroughness had fortified this plain with great concrete structures, all arranged on a mutually co-operating plan. Some of the concretes were veritable fortresses. There is a certain irony in the rumour that a

CAPT. S. B. TUBBS.
Officer Commanding D Company.

CAPT. L. DUDBRIDGE,
M.C. AND BAR.
Officer Commanding D Company.

large amount of the concrete used had come from British firms through neutral countries. The plain itself was a desolate pock-marked area, ripped to pieces by gun fire almost since the commencement of the War. All drainage was destroyed and the advent of rain at once turned the whole place into one vast bog of pestilential slime and filth. It was across this plain that the advance on Passchendaele had to be made. Duckboard tracks were laid and along these the men moved in single file. To slip off these tracks, as sometimes happened at night, often meant drowning in slime ; to remain on them was almost as perilous since the German guns had every track taped.

The conditions of the mud in this and other areas is trenchantly illustrated by the following story. A British Tommy was picking his way along a duckboard track when, ever alive to the possibility of a souvenir, he espied an Australian hat lying in the mud. Stooping to pick it up, he was surprised that it resisted his efforts : the reason, he soon discovered, was that it was held down by the strap which went under the chin of its owner, whose eyes were just visible above the slush. Getting a firm foothold, he dived his arms into the mud and under the other's armpits and tried to drag him out. " Steady does it, Tommy," spluttered the Australian, through a welter of slush, " I'm on a horse."

The Battalion moved first to Buysscheure area and then to Watou area, and on August 21st it went up the line to the support trenches in Warwick Farm, east of the big Wieltje Dugout which was Brigade Headquarters and advanced Field Ambulance dressing station.

On August 22nd the Brigade attacked with the Oxfords on the left and the Bucks on the right. The Glosters were in support. At the last moment, the orders for the Glosters were altered and two Companies were ordered to move into position at Zero behind the Oxfords and two behind the Bucks. Headquarters was at Call Reserve, a big German concrete that had been captured. The Oxfords were commanded by Lt.-Col. R. H. Wetherall, a young regular officer of the Gloucester Regiment, the Bucks by a very cheery officer of the Black Watch Territorials, by name, Lt.-Col. J. Muir.

Both Battalions made a magnificent advance which carried them right forward almost to their limits. But, as so often happened, the losses were so great that it was impossible to hold the farthest objectives, and they were pushed back fighting hard. Soon D Company was despatched to reinforce the left, and B Company the right. While moving up with D Company, gallant Seymour Tubbs was killed leading his men.

The expression, " he was loved by everyone," became rather the convention of the day ; but in the case of Capt. Tubbs, it was literally true, because he possessed in an unusual degree the gift for friendship. Wherever he was, there radiated a warmth of happy comradeship ; a capable and gallant officer, a perfect sportsman, a delightful companion, he could ill be spared.

In the centre of the Oxfords' advance was a grim and giant concrete fortress called Pond Farm, manned by fifty picked German machine-gunners with five guns. This fortress had resisted the assaults of no less than five Divisions in previous fighting. At 12 noon, two platoons attacked it unsuccessfully after a hurricane bombardment. Two platoons from C Company were then sent up and these, together with D Company, stormed the concrete fortress with great dash, killing or capturing its entire garrison. The losses were heavy : 2nd Lieuts. Davis and Blythe and 16 other ranks were killed, and 2nd Lieut. Ross Jenkins and 51 other ranks were wounded and one other was missing.

During the night there was an unfortunate incident. The garrison was small and no other officer of the Glosters left, and one of another unit detailed to take command did not arrive. A fierce German counter-attack, launched at the right, was beaten off by the Bucks with D Company, but swerving away, it swept on to the flank and rear of Pond Farm and recaptured it. It was a great pity, but the memory of the

POND FARM, YPRES—AUGUST 1917.

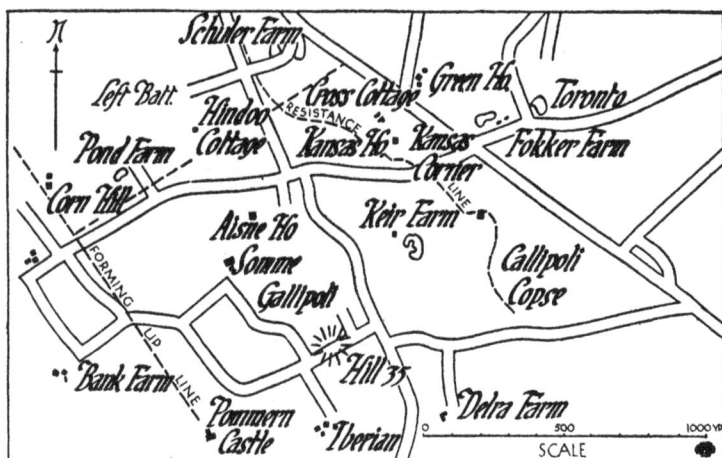

Pond Farm.

gallant attack which captured the fortress wipes out any small stain caused by its weak garrison losing it. Next day it was easily recaptured.

On the right flank D Company, under command of Lieut. Johnston, was soon sent forward to support the Bucks and detailed to hold and consolidate a line just west of Hill 35. This gallant Scotch officer, helped by his men, performed deeds of valour : he consolidated his line, roped in stragglers from another Division and put them in position, extended his line to get into touch right and left, and beat off every counter-attack. His report to the Commanding Officer at Call Reserve, written under heavy shell fire in the open, was the most cheerful document ever penned. He was highly commended by Lt.-Col. Muir, and sent to Corps Headquarters to give an account of the fight. He was recommended for the D.S.O. and was awarded the M.C. He is perhaps best described as one who was just as happy in a fight as at a tea party surrounded by pretty girls.

The Battalion was relieved by the 2/6th Glosters and moved to Red Rose Camp for refitting.

On August 28th Lieut. Wooster and a party of twenty-five reported for duty as auxiliary stretcher bearers, to the very gallant O.C. Advanced Field Ambulance, Col. Scott-Williamson, D.S.O., who had twice gone into No Man's Land with a red cross flag and had rescued a number of wounded who might otherwise have died a lingering death. He persuaded Frank Wooster to put on a brassard and to accompany his party on a third journey. This time, however, the Germans turned nasty and marched them in. There was great anxiety for Wooster's safety, but happily he is still alive to tell the tale. On August 30th, the Battalion moved into Brigade support on the Canal Bank near the Dead End. A good deal of swimming was indulged in here until it was found that broken bottles were poor things to step on bare-footed, and that dead horses make unpleasant bath salts.

About this time the Battalion was warned for an attack on Gallipoli and Hill 35 and practices were carried out on a marked course. No one who was acquainted with the Ypres fighting, cared for these single battalion attacks on a small front, for directly the Germans located where the disturbance was, they concentrated every available weapon of war on to the spot. Thus the result was always a great sacrifice of life and no appreciable gain. The evening before the Battalion went up, the Commanding Officer was holding a final conference of Company Commanders when a well-groomed Major of the Army Staff, complete with eye-glass, rolled in and asked for the Commanding Officer's opinion of this particular form of fighting. The Commanding Officer took him firmly outside and told him exactly what he did think. The Staff Officer then informed the Commanding Officer that all other Commanding Officers had expressed a similar opinion, but that Col. Collett had put the matter a great deal more forcibly. Whether these opinions ever reached the Higher Command is not known, but on taking over the line in Somme Concrete and facing Hill 35, to the Battalion's intense relief, the attack was cancelled. Thankfully relieved that the attack was off, all ranks worked like niggers to improve the line and were finally taken out by the 55th Division. Buses took the troops to Watou No. 3 Area and then a march landed them at Worm Houldt where resting and refitting were the order of the day.

CHAPTER VIII

BACK TO ARRAS

THE " Gallipoli scare," as this meditated attack may well be called, occurred in the early days of September 1917. After the affair had been cancelled on the 12th, the men were chiefly occupied in cleaning up by day and in digging trenches by night for the next two or three days. On the 18th, the Battalion entrained for Aubigny, a six-hours' journey, and on arriving there it marched to Duisans. Nothing of any note occurred until October 4th when it again went into the line, taking over a part of Greenland Hill Sector in the St. Nicholas Area.

C Company under Capt. Badcock was ordered to make a raid. His raiding party of about sixty went out of the line to train and the attack took place on October 23rd. The letter which Capt. Badcock wrote home after the raid is worth reproducing not only because it gives graphic details of the fight, but because, whatever may be written and thought to the contrary, it shows that the men who fought preserved their instinct for humaneness and their sense of decency, under the most revolting conditions.

" My ——,

" I have not written for some time. I have done a raid show. It did not go badly : we collared some prisoners, one machine-gun, and did in about 20. It was the most disgusting shambles I have ever seen. The wretched Germans were simply mad with fright and it seemed sheer butchery, all poor youths of eighteen

74

CAPT. J. H. E. RICKERBY, M.C.
Officer Commanding A Company.

CAPT. M. F. BADCOCK, M.C.
Officer Commanding C Company.

and nineteen. We got 10 prisoners, but 6 were killed going across No Man's Land by their own shells; one fool surrendered to me and thrust at me with his bayonet; it went through my trousers, tore my pants, and never touched me. There was nothing to do but to shoot him. It's the first life I have ever taken in this war to my certain knowledge and it was beastly. We did not have a single fellow killed, only four slightly wounded and all got in safe, so it was a success. Our fellows absolutely saw red and we had a job to stop the killing. We blew up three of their dugouts, which they would not come out of, so I suppose they were buried and suffocated. The sight of us, black hats, black hands and faces, black bayonets and darkness, only white flaring Verey lights and the unceasing crash of our shells on their support lines, made it seem pretty awful.

" Well, we were lucky to have whole skins and people seem fairly pleased, so I suppose it's alright, still I don't want to do another for a week or two. Radford, my second in command and Ross Jenkins were simply fine and did their jobs well. I sat in comparative safety, blowing whistles and playing with coloured lights and passing shivering boys out over the parapet as prisoners. Poor kids, all offering me and the men watches, money and papers and feverishly saying, ' Kamerad English, ver goot not shoot.' The man with the machine-gun was crying with his head wrapped up in a great coat. We killed one German officer who tried to surrender and then pulled out a pistol and fired.

" The German regiment had just come down from Ypres where it had had no end of a hammering, and there was no spirit left in it. If they have come down here for a rest, heaven help them, for our Division is giving them none. . . . The German artillery went mad, I think, and regardless of their own men being there as well as ours, shelled and killed their own front line. The guns had already blown the trench flat and must have buried a good part of the garrison. Well, I'm glad I'm not a Fritz. . . ."

After the raid the Battalion was relieved by the 2/8th Warwicks and went into Divisional Reserve at Arras, being billetted in the Levis Barracks.

About this time the Brigade formed a School of Instruction at Arras under command of Major Bennett of the Oxfords ; and to this School each battalion sent a platoon. After eight days' training, a competition was held. It speaks well for the efficiency of the 2/5th that out of the four platoons sent, three won the first prize and the other the second. 2nd Lieuts. Downing, Ross Jenkins and Welch were the winning Platoon Commanders. The Brigadier told Major Bennett that he was surprised that the Glosters appeared to be the best trained unit in the Brigade, but the Glosters had their own opinion on this.

On November 9th the Battalion relieved the 2/8th Worcesters in the Chemical Works Sector. Poor Lieut. Dodgshon was killed here. He had only just joined and had entertained large crowds in Arras just previously with his wonderful conjuring tricks.

About this time, the Commanding Officer with Capt. Rickerby and an Orderly Sergeant went round to reconnoitre an additional piece of line that it was thought the Battalion would have to take over. While returning up a communication trench a hurricane bombardment opened on them ; they bolted back some 200 yards to a Trench Mortar dugout they had just been shown. How they got there is still a mystery, as the trench was blown to pieces. However, Providence engineers strange vagaries of fortune, and the lucky ones celebrated their deliverance in a much appreciated whisky and soda.

While the Battalion was on the Arras Front Capt. Barnes rejoined. He was a devoted student of Omar Khayyam, and always carried a red pocket edition of the Rubaiyat. At Arras on one occasion he was acting Adjutant and the men were engaged in battalion drill, when they suddenly tied themselves into knots so badly that the Commanding Officer had to re-form them on markers. He was horrified to see Barnes produce a small red book, which he took to be a drill manual. Thinking he must have given a wrong order, he asked Barnes what the drill book said. " Oh no, sir," came the reply, " I was only looking to see what old Omar would have said about it." Barnes always said that he was the world's worst soldier, but others don't agree, though they would never have given him full marks for his turn out.

At the end of November a move was made to the Cambrai Front, where General Byng had achieved a notable advance. All were sorry to leave Sir Charles Ferguson's Corps, because they realised that he was a general who took a great personal interest in everyone under his command. Sir Charles was often round the line and, on one occasion, just when the Italians were giving way badly, he asked the Commanding Officer who was the officer with the M.C. and the Italian Medal he had just seen down the trench. It was Capt. Rickerby and Sir Charles went on, " I don't think he is very pleased with his Italian friends at the moment because he asked me if he could take off his Italian ribbon." That was a typical remark of one of the most gallant officers in the Battalion. Later, in March 1918, when the British were being driven in on the St. Quentin Front, he refused to go back, though wounded, and died fighting.

The Battalion moved by train to Royaucourt and then by bus to Fins, where it arrived at 6 p.m. Everyone there was in a state of intense excitement as the enemy had broken through and the Battalion expected every moment to be ordered into action. It moved at midnight to Gonnelieu and supported the 3rd Guards Brigade which had been fighting continuously for eight days. It remained in close support until the following night when orders were received to move through Villers Plouich to a map reference behind Welsh Ridge and await orders. The road was a shambles, but the objective was reached without much loss. While awaiting orders, Capt. Dudbridge reported that he had halted his Company in a sunken road, so the Commanding Officer proceeded with him to see the position. When nearly there a terrific explosion occurred, blowing both over. A night-flying aeroplane had dropped a bomb at a venture and had hit an ammunition dump, which stood on the top of the bank above D Company's position. D Company's casualties were 16 killed and 53 wounded, and the gunners near by suffered heavily in men and horses. Just as this disaster occurred, orders arrived from Brigade to take up a position on Welsh Ridge. Instinct told the Commanding Officer that the present spot was likely to prove a very unhealthy one, so orders were quickly issued to move companies to their allotted positions. The movement had to be carried out in inky darkness and without guides, so there was a certain amount of hold up. Capt. Gray remained with Headquarters while the Commanding Officer led the foremost company through the Hindenburg wire ; the rest of the Battalion followed and the new positions were found. No sooner had the sunken road been cleared than a terrific bombardment opened on the spot the Battalion had just left. Capt. Gray with Headquarters only barely missed it.

At dawn the enemy attacked La Vacquerie, driving in the Warwicks and Glosters. That morning Lieut. W. J. Pearce, one of Gloucester's best footballers, was killed.

Even under such circumstances as these, war has its funny side. Sergt. Dobbs relates that the Battalion at the time was so much under strength that the sanitary men amongst others were requisitioned for duty in the firing line. It happened that one of these men, very much resembling " Old Bill," was wounded in the face by a piece of shrapnel. For a long time he stoutly refused to have his face bandaged. At last he consented but only on condition that his false teeth, which he treasured apparently more than anything else, were retrieved. It was, however, found that his dentals had been shattered into fragments and the news had

BATTALION PARADE—1915.

SOME OF D COMPANY N.C.O.'S IN FIGHTING ORDER.

to be broken to him gently. He was inconsolable until he was assured that the Army Authorities would provide him with a perfectly good new set free of charge.

An urgent order, repeated three times, was received on the 18th to attack La Vacquerie, but, to the relief of everyone, it turned out to be a mistake.

Shortly afterwards, the Warwicks' line was broken into by a hostile bombing attack. Capt. Dudbridge, who was on the right, organised, on his own initiative, a counter bombing attack and succeeded in re-establishing the line. This little action proved that D Company, under the inspiring leadership of Capt. Dudbridge, had lost none of its morale, in spite of the disaster in the sunken road which might well have shaken the Company to pieces. Capt. Dudbridge and Lieut. Radford were awarded a stout-hearted M.C. apiece, and Pte. W. A. Davis gained the M.M.

On December 5th the Battalion moved to Villers Plouich, and on the 7th into the line near Corner Work. The former place was still a shambles and was soaked with phosgene gas, necessitating the constant wearing of gas masks. Trophies, left by retiring troops, were picked up galore and the messes replenished themselves to their heart's content. Relief came on December 10th and a move was made into huts in Havrincourt Wood. After the Battalion had left the line, the Commanding Officer followed with a guide who was meant to take him to billets. The guide, however, missed the way and added an unnecessary four miles to the journey. The Commanding Officer's remarks to the guide and afterwards about him are unprintable. Capt. Beloe, however, regaled him with the largest whisky and soda a Commanding Officer ever negotiated, and all was well.

It was here that the news reached the Battalion of Col. Balfour's death. He had been sniped while inspecting his wire at dawn. His death cast a gloom over the unit which he had commanded with so much distinction and by which he was so much appreciated and loved.

On December 16th, 1,000 yards of line opposite La Vacquerie was taken over. The battle had by now quietened down and consolidation was the main occupation.

2nd Lieut. Lake was sent out on patrol one night and from his report he must have wandered right round La Vacquerie. He had the heart of a lion and though the information gained was not of great value, he must have surprised many a German sentry. In its way it was a brilliant little piece of work.

Just inside this line a big gun had been left, and on the night of the 18th a Major appeared with sixty men in order to salve it. The gun moved a little and then sank into the soft ground. The Major was desolate, but a stiff " binder " and the help of the Glosters' Reserve Company put new spirit into him. The monster was eventually pulled into the hard road and taken away. The Major, good soul, finished the Headquarters' supply of whisky and then said the gun cost £10,000, so perhaps it was worth it.

On the 20th the Battalion was in Brigade Reserve in Havrincourt Wood. Aeroplanes were unceasing in their attentions. Once, when Brig.-Gen. White was conferring with his commanding officers, an enemy plane came along dropping bombs, each one nearer the hut in which the conference was taking place. Everyone looked to see what the Brigadier would do. He merely went on with his dissertation, as the last bomb but one dropped 100 yards short of the hut and the last one 100 yards beyond it. What a lovely bag that young German flyer had missed !

On the 24th the Battalion entrained for Cappy behind the Somme Front and was billetted in huts. Snow enveloped the countryside and there were some realistic bombing fights with snow balls. There were no casualties. A further move was made to Rosieres on the 29th where the official Xmas Dinner was held, a convivial affair at which the Commanding Officer and others are expected to drink an exaggerated number of toasts.

About this time, Capt. Beloe and Capt. Bicknell were awarded the M.C.

On January 6th the Battalion took over from the French at Mesnil. The weather was cold and wet and the Brigade was engaged in trench duties and in other work at Fresnoy and Maissemy.

The nature of the country in this part of France is open and undulating, giving from the rising ground wide, distant views, and being entirely dominated by the great Cathedral of St. Quentin. At this time General Headquarters must have known that the Germans were preparing for a great and decisive attack, since numerous divisions were known to have been sent to the Western Front after the recent collapse of Russia as well as others from Italy and Roumania. It has, in fact, been estimated that the German Army on this front received reinforcements from these sources to the tune of 19,000 officers and 600,000 other ranks. Where the attack would be launched was, of course, unknown.

A new system of defences was adopted by General Headquarters. There were to be three distinct areas of defence— a Forward, a Battle, and a Rear Zone. The Forward Zone was to consist of a line of outposts with strongly fortified redoubts on the rising ground behind. These redoubts, though from 500 to 1,500 yards apart, were not connected up by any system of trenches but a single line of barbed wire with a machine-gun post here and there. The Redoubts and the machine-gun forts were sited so that they could sweep with converging fire all the intervening low-lying ground. The depth of the Forward Zone was about 3,000 yards and its purpose was to break up and disorganise the leading troops of the German assault.

Behind this came the Battle Zone, consisting also of Redoubts but without the line of outposts.

The last line was the Rear Zone, some two miles behind the Battle Zone and consisting of a double line of trenches.

So far as the 184th was concerned, the forward battalion held a line of posts north of Fayet with a strong point at

Enghien Redoubt. These posts were very lightly held and were at distances of approximately 100 yards. The support Battalion held that part of the Battle Zone which lay along the front of Holnon Wood. The reserve battalion was some miles behind at a village called Ugny.

The holding of such an extended line so lightly was probably a necessity, but to say the least of it, it was audacious.

On January 26th the Battalion made a move into huts at Vaux, and on the 28th digging in the Battle Zone commenced.

During February and the early part of March, the Glosters took their turn in these various positions and very hard work was put in, strengthening and improving them, so that ultimately the Brigade front began to look so strong from the Enghien Redoubt and the Battle Zone that it seemed like suicide for anyone to attack it. How wide these convictions were of the mark was shown later when the Germans made their final onslaught.

About this time Major Gilbert Beloe went on leave, and was subsequently struck off the strength on April 11th, 1918. He was appointed Adjutant while the Battalion was on Salisbury Plain, and acted in this capacity until, on becoming Second in Command, he was relieved of that duty by Capt. Gray in June 1917. He was most efficient in all the duties pertaining to an adjutant, and when later greater demands were made upon his executive skill, as acting Commanding Officer in the absence of the Commanding Officer, he was equally successful. He did much while with the Battalion to make the machinery work smoothly and efficiently.

During one tour in the forward position, an outpost was attacked by three parties and practically surrounded, but it gallantly beat off the attackers. On another occasion, in a mist, a post was attacked and beaten off by Cpl. Gapper, who captured a German Sergeant Major and three others. From these prisoners important information was obtained, and Cpl. Gapper was awarded the M.M.

MAJOR G. C. BELOE, M.C.
Adjutant, May 1916—July 1917.

CAPT. H. V. GRAY, M.C.
Adjutant, July 1917—November 1918.

On yet another occasion the Commanding Officer was with Lt.-Col. Davidson, on the Glosters' extreme right, when the Germans, in a thick mist, walked over, thinking that the outpost line had been evacuated. It was disconcerting for the Commanding Officer to find himself thus completely out of touch with the main part of his sector. However the machine-gunners and riflemen at that point made good shooting on the target offered them, and the interlopers bolted back much more quickly than they had approached— they must have paid quite a price for that little jaunt.

Major Day recounts an experience that gives a good idea of the open character of operations on this front, so different from the trench life of the Fauquissart Sector.

Major Day was in command of B Company at Gricourt with A Company on his left. Running at right angles from his front and right across to the German line was a track that had once been a road. He had established a Lewis gun post at the point where the track met his line. On visiting the post one morning at 2 a.m. he was informed that A Company's patrol had been seen coming down the track from the direction of the German lines. It had halted, he was told, at B Company's wire and had then moved off. On the next night similar information was reported to him. On making enquiries from A Company it became quite clear that the patrol was in reality a German one. Just before dawn Major Day went into No Man's Land to the point indicated and there found distinct signs of a track made by a number of men walking in single file. As the patrol was proved to be an enemy one, and as the same point on his wire had been visited on successive nights, he suspected that a raid was contemplated.

He got Major Davis, R.E., to make him a mobile charge and with this he set up a booby trap with a long trip wire attached to the pin so that the charge would explode directly anyone blundered into the trip wire. It was arranged that when the charge exploded machine and Lewis gunners were to open fire for two minutes and then a party was to rush out to bring in wounded and prisoners. The trap was in position at 7 p.m. At midnight an A Company patrol ran into a strong German party about 100 yards away from the trap ; there was a good deal of shouting and firing. Soon after Major Day got wind that the German party was moving along the wire but still well to the left of the trap. To drive the enemy towards the trap he decided to use rifle grenades. These he dropped over on the left of the Germans and the ruse was immediately successful as they started moving to the right. They came nearer and nearer, the grenades all the time dropping just on their left, until they were within 25 yards of the trap. Just when hopes were running high and everyone was ready to give them a warm reception, they suddenly turned away and broke across No Man's Land for home—and so what promised to be a most successful affair was nipped in the bud. Everyone was much disappointed. It had, however, taught the Germans that other people besides themselves were wide awake, and they showed no further disposition to repeat their visits.

On March 10th the Battalion was relieved by the 2/4th Berks, commanded by Col. Dimmer, V.C., and went into reserve at Ugny, where it was occupied in cleaning up and training.

On the 17th Lt.-Col. G. F. Collett said farewell and handed over the command to Lt.-Col. A. B. Lawson, 11th Hussars.

Col. Collett had been with the Battalion since April 1917, and had commanded it since June 29th of that year. He had thus had time to get to know his officers and men and they on their part had had the opportunity to prove his worth, since it was under his command that many of their most strenuous days were lived. Col. Collett came to the 2/5th with a long experience of soldiering behind him ; his knowledge of tactics and his exceptional eye for country were assets of the utmost value under the conditions that obtained at the time. More than that, having been a

Territorial in pre-war days, he understood the mentality of the civilian soldier ; his bonhomie and geniality made him the friend as well as the commanding officer of the Battalion, and it was no mere convention that prompted all the officers and men to turn out en masse to wish him good-bye.

CHAPTER IX

THE BIG PUSH (MARCH 21ST–31ST, 1918)

ON March 18th the Battalion relieved the 2/4th Oxfords and took over the defences of Holnon Wood, one of the strong points in the Battle Zone. The wood lies on high ground about half a mile west of Holnon village and from its eastern outskirts gives extensive views of the ground stretching forward to the German lines. Being in support and some 5,000 yards from the front line, the Battalion lived in Attilly Huts on the west edge of the Wood and worked on the defences during the day.

Speculation had for a long time been rife as to the contemplated German attack. As usual, the incurable optimists said that it would never materialise, but in a raid made by the Royal Warwickshires, prisoners had been captured who stated positively that the barrage would open at 5 a.m. on March 21st, and that the attack would be launched at 10 a.m. on that day. Even then it was thought that this news might be a piece of false information passed on for the purpose of misleading the Allies. However, on the evening of the 20th, a message from Brigade to the effect that a captured German airman had stated that the attack was to commence at dawn was sent out to companies with instructions to be prepared to move to battle stations immediately on receipt of orders to that effect.

These rumours proved to be no fiction, for at 4.30 a.m. on the 21st a terrific bombardment of high explosives and gas shells opened on the battery positions and the defences of the wood.

86

MESSAGES AND SIGNALS.

Prefix . Code .. .... m.	Words	Charge	This message is on a/o of:	Recd. at................m.
Office of Origin and Service Instructions.				Date........................
....	Sent		...............................Service.	From ....
Priority	At.....................m.			
....	To			
....	By		(Signature of " Franking Officer.")	By ....

TO	{	8 Cy		m J. Cy		

Sender's Number.	Day of Month.	In reply to Number.	
* A 1	21		A A A

MAN BATTLE STATIONS

From	184 Bde			
Place				
Time				

The above may be forwarded as now corrected.   **(Z)**   John Hunter

....

Censor.   Signature of Address or person authorized to telegraph in his name.

* This line should be erased if not required.

750,000. W 2186—M509. H. W. & V., Ld. 6/16.

"MAN BATTLE STATIONS"
(Copy of the original message)

Pieces of shells hurtled through the air ; trees came crashing down ; shells hit the huts ; guns were knocked out ; and the whole place reeked of gas. It was found almost at once that every telephone line had been broken, so that there was no chance of getting any information or orders as to the situation from Brigade. Linesmen were sent out to repair the lines and frantic calls were kept up from the signallers' hut ; runners were despatched to ask for information and orders. After what seemed an age connection was re-established with an Artillery Brigade, and information came through that there was a message from Brigade Headquarters to the 2/5th Glosters. It read the ominous words, " Man battle positions." It was now 4.45 a.m. and five minutes later the Battalion was on the move. The journey to the battle positions was a matter of several hundred yards through the wood and over an area soaked with gas shells and high explosives. That only very few casualties were suffered during the actual journey is one of those miracles that defeat explanation.

The Battalion's dispositions in the Battle Zone were as follows : A and B Companies held the eastern defences of the Redoubt—A on the left front under Capt. Rickerby, B on the right front under Lieut. Arnott ; C Company under Lieut. Howell held the northern defences and was designated as the counter-attack Company ; D Company under Capt. Dudbridge was in support.

The intense bombardment continued for more than four hours and with a heavy mist prevailing until midday, (afterwards found to be partly artificial) it was impossible to form any idea as to what was happening in front. When the mist cleared it was seen that the Germans had passed through the Forward Zone and had formed a line about 500 yards in front of the Battle Zone and were bringing up trench mortars and field guns. With these they fired over open sights and inflicted many casualties, but machine-gun and rifle fire prevented them from making any further advance during daylight. Later in the day Capt. Gray did heroic work in making his way from Battalion Headquarters under continuous shell fire to visit the Companies in their battle positions.

After dark enemy patrols became very active, one patrol entering the trenches between A and B Companies and bombing towards B Company's strong point. It was, however, driven out. Lieut. Arnott had a very anxious night and reported at midnight that the Germans were working round his right flank. During this difficult period in which he did such good work Lieut. Arnott was unfortunately killed by a shell when visiting one of his posts.

What did actually occur in the Forward Zone on March 21st is set out in a summary of the events written by Lt.-Gen. Sir Ivor Maxse, commanding 18th Corps

" 2/8th Worcesters, 2/4th Oxfords and Bucks, and 2/5th Gordon Highlanders were holding a front of 6,000 yards and occupied ground to a depth of 1,500 yards in rear of their outposts. These heroic battalions were first subjected to an intensive bombardment by all calibres of guns and trench mortars for five hours and were then overwhelmed by not less than three German divisions which assaulted at 10 a.m. The fog prevented S.O.S. rockets from being seen and so prevented the artillery and machine-gun section from co-operating by firing on distant targets. The Redoubt remained in telephonic communication with Corps Headquarters by means of a buried cable till 4.10 p.m. At that hour the garrisons were told that they might cut their way out at night, but except for a few odd men no one returned from the three battalions whose duty it was to hold the Forward Zone. They simply fought it out on the spot and their heroism will live for ever in the annals of their regiments. . . . Details are lacking but we know that they held up three divisions throughout the whole day and prevented the enemy from assaulting the Battle Zone of the 61st Division."

This information was not of course known at the time by those holding the Battle Zone.

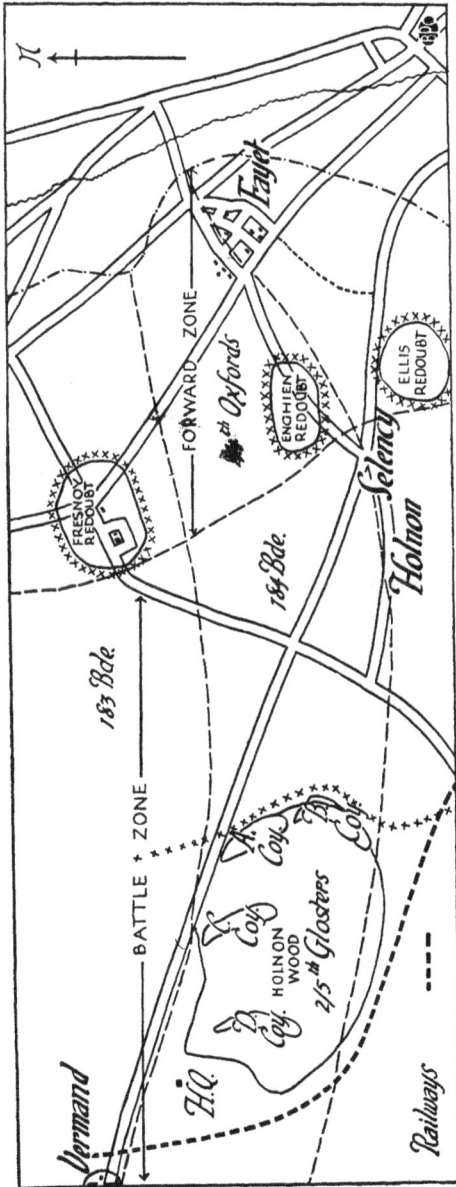

The St. Quentin Front, showing Front Line and Battle positions on March 21st, 1918.

The morning of the 22nd was misty until about 10 a.m., again making it impossible to gauge the situation. When the mist cleared it was found that small parties of Germans with machine-guns had worked their way down the Vermand road in rear of our support positions and were causing casualties to Battalion Headquarters and D Company.

At 9 a.m. an intensive bombardment had been again opened and several attacks were made on C Company's position. These were repelled, but during one of them Lieut. Howell was mortally wounded.

The position of the whole Battalion after midday was getting desperate as the Germans were seen assembling on the high ground east of Vermand, making it clear that the Battle Zone on the left had fallen and that in a few hours the Battalion would be surrounded.

At 3.30 p.m. a message from Brigade ordered a withdrawal to the rear zone trenches in front of Beauvois. Enemy aeroplanes were now coming over in large numbers, flying very low and enfilading the infantry ; one came down which was captured with its pilot.

For the withdrawal of the Battalion, D Company was ordered to remain in position to give covering fire, while the other companies moved back. When later D Company received its orders to move it had to fight a stiff rearguard action and was at the same time subjected to enfilading fire from machine-guns in Attilly on its right. Owing, however, to the skill with which Capt. Dudbridge manipulated his troops and to the heroism of all ranks, the Company ultimately joined the Battalion at Beauvois. To prevent Battalion Headquarters from being cut off Capt. Barnes, with a few Headquarter details, had been ordered to keep the enemy at bay. Capt. Barnes and his party were surrounded and nearly all were either killed or captured : they succeeded, however, in delaying the Germans long enough to enable the remainder of Headquarters to get away.

The uncompleted trenches at Beauvois, shallow and meagrely wired, were manned about 5 p.m. Much-needed ammunition was replenished from a large dump on the Beauvois road.

About 6 p.m. large numbers of Germans were seen advancing out of Holnon Wood and moving in attack formation over the flat ground. After a short sharp bombardment, the attack was launched but was held up by the wire, scanty as it was. It was during this bombardment that Capt. Rickerby was hit by a shell and died of his wounds.

Capt. Rickerby's death was a disaster to the Battalion and a great personal loss to his many friends. He had served with the Battalion from its infancy, had taken a distinguished part in many of its most notable achievements and had added lustre to its fame. He was of a type to whom clean life and hard living are a part of a deep religion. To these attributes he added a capacity for detail and an instinct for soldiering that made him a leader among others. Possessing a stern sense of duty and full of the joy of living, yet completely regardless of death, he was the ideal Company Commander.

March 22nd had taken heavy toll of the Battalion, for besides Capt. Rickerby, Lieut. Nurse had been killed and Lieuts. Stirling and Russell and 2nd Lieuts. Crossman and Hazell wounded.

This episode of the fighting has been immortalised by Sir Arthur Conan Doyle in *The British Campaign in France and Flanders, January to July*, 1918. In it he speaks of the tenacity and determination of the 2/5th Glosters, and mentions the names of Lt.-Col. Lawson, Capt. Rickerby and Capt. Dudbridge.

At midnight on the 22nd/23rd the Royal Berks informed the Commanding Officer that they were retiring to Voyennes. As ammunition was running low and the Germans were known to be working round the Battalion's right flank, he decided to withdraw before daylight. Intimate knowledge of the country enabled the Battalion to get away undetected.

Thus the three Defensive Zones upon which so much labour had been spent fell into the hands of the enemy in less that forty-eight hours' fighting, and what happened on the small sector defended by the 2/5th Glosters happened on the entire front of the 5th Army and in fact, the 3rd Army on its left fared very little better.

The line held by the 5th Army on March 21st was forty-two miles in length and was defended by eleven divisions in the line, one in reserve, together with two cavalry divisions. Two other divisions normally attached to the 5th Army were under direct orders of General Headquarters. Compared with this the 3rd Army held twenty-six and a half miles with ten divisions in the line and seven in support. It was estimated that it would take seventy-two hours for reinforc-ing divisions to arrive and then only one at a time, while French divisions could only have arrived minus guns and transport.

Against the 5th Army were nearly four times as many Germans, consisting of specially trained and picked troops, backed up by an enormous preponderance in the matter of artillery.

After the retreat from the St. Quentin Sector, the Battalion was kept continuously on the move. On the morning of the 24th it marched to Voyennes and thence to Langue-voisin where a sorely needed meal was obtained ; it then moved on to Billancourt and later returned to Langue-voisin for the night. Early next morning the Germans were reported to have captured Ham and to be moving on Nesle. The Battalion was, therefore, ordered to cover the crossing of the Du Nord Canal at Buverchy. Positions had no sooner been taken up than a fresh move was made to defend the crossing at Breuil. C Company crossed the canal and was advancing in open order to take up a position on the right flank, when it was enfiladed by an enemy machine-gun, Lieut. Lake who was gallantly leading the Company being killed. 2nd Lieut. Fothergill was also killed about this time and Lieut. Rowlands wounded. As the Germans appeared in great numbers C Company was withdrawn. The line of the canal bank was defended and trenches were dug in rear of the village and occupied.

On the morning of the 25th the Germans heavily bombarded the canal bank and put a machine-gun barrage on the village, which lasted for more than an hour. They then attempted to cross but were easily stopped by rifle and Lewis gun fire. During the day the Germans established a Headquarters in a farmhouse some 600 yards north-west of the village and snipers had a busy time dealing with the mounted orderlies who were seen going to and from it. One of D Company's Lewis gunners got into a high building from which he could see Germans massing in a flat field beyond the canal. All the Company's guns were, therefore, taken to this building and heavy losses were inflicted on the assembling troops.

About 2 p.m. the Commanding Officer was sent for to command the Brigade and Major Day was left in charge of the Battalion. He had a trying time as matters soon began to get unpleasant. He dealt, however, with each problem as it arose, coolly and effectively. About 4 p.m. the break came ; the French troops on the right were seen to be retiring and the Germans to be crossing the canal at Buverchy, deploying and working round the Glosters' right flank. A defensive right flank was thrown out to hold up the enemy, while the Battalion withdrew on Cressy. During this operation 2nd Lieuts. Perkins, Downing and Bugler were wounded. At midnight orders were received to move to Roye. This journey was followed by a further one to Mezieres along the Roye–Amiens road. The whole British army appeared to be on the move and the road was indescribably congested with troops, guns, limbers and wagons.

Mezieres was reached at 11 a.m. The Battalion was very much depleted and very tired, so the afternoon was given over to as much rest as was possible. Fortunately some good champagne was unearthed in the village.

At 6 p.m. orders were received to take up positions north-west of Quesnil where a line of posts was dug.

The night 26th/27th was fairly quiet and on the morning of the 27th the posts were strengthened and extended towards

Quesnil Wood. It was here that touch was again made with the Brigade Artillery under the command of Major W. H. Taylor, and just when it was expected that the enemy would renew the attack, the order came to vacate this position. To the surprise and dismay of the Battalion motor omnibuses were waiting on the main road. British troops were always suspicious of these contrivances as they generally meant a quick way of getting to a nasty job. The present instance was no exception since the Battalion had no sooner arrived at Marcelcave than it received orders to partake in an attack on Lamotte. The attack appeared so utterly hopeless that the Divisional General appealed to Corps to cancel the order, but without avail.

The attack started at 12 noon with A Company on the right, D on the left and C in support (B Company not having yet arrived). There was no artillery to give a barrage and the only assistance given to the infantry was supplied by an aeroplane that fired a machine-gun at the enemy. It seemed obvious at the start of the attack that the Battalion would be wiped out as the gently rising ground afforded no cover and gave an uninterrupted field of fire to the enemy. The troops were allowed to get half way to their objective with practically no opposition and then it seemed as though all the machine-guns in the German Army had opened fire together. The men, however, held firm and dug themselves in with intrenching tools ; it had to be done lying flat on the ground under a murderous fire. The enemy's position was found to be strongly held and the place of deployment was swept by machine-gun fire ; the attack was thus, from its commencement, doomed to failure and the Battalion suffered 200 casualties. Orders were given to withdraw on Marcelcave and in the withdrawal further casualties were suffered including Lieut. Knight wounded and Lieut. Gallagher missing.

At 2 p.m. the same afternoon the Battalion was ordered to extend the line in the railway cutting in front of Marcelcave. The enemy, by this time, had brought up large quantities of artillery which shelled the position heavily till 6 p.m., when an attack was launched and the Germans penetrated the trenches to the south-west of the village. Enemy machine-guns were then able to enfilade the railway bank, which made it an impossible place in which to remain.

Orders to withdraw and to dig in 1,000 yards west of the village on the outskirts of the Aerodrome and across the railway line Marcelcave–Villers-Bretonneux followed. It was here that Colonel Pagan joined as Commander of the 184th Brigade. The position was now desperate. The Battalion was reduced to about 150 tired men ; these men were holding a thin line of posts ten miles in front of Amiens with no supports of any kind. Had the Germans attacked during the next three days Amiens was theirs. Happily for the Glosters and the Allied cause they did not move.

Throughout the entire night 28th/29th the Battalion dug in and when morning came it was found that there was another gap in the line on the left of the Brigade front, so another move had to be made to fill it and posts again had to be dug.

The Germans had now dug themselves in on the slight ridge in front of the village and their artillery shelled the British posts throughout the day. Four machine-guns, manned by Canadians, were sent up to reinforce the Battalion. They were ordered to fire as much ammunition as they could spare in order to deceive the enemy as to the numerical strength of the defence. During enemy shelling at this time Major Day and Capt. Dudbridge were wounded. It is worth mentioning that D Company's Headquarters were, on this occasion, situated in the cemetery, showing a nice sense of adaptation. The Battalion held on to the position through the night 29th/30th and was relieved on the morning of the 31st by Australians.

This period from March 21st, 1918, was the most critical one that the Glosters ever went through. Throughout the whole of this terrible experience Col. Lawson was in command, either of the Battalion or the Brigade ; he displayed the utmost bravery, courage and coolness. A great tribute, too, must be paid the officers and men, who performed prodigies of endurance, fighting by day, marching and digging by night, without ever getting a proper meal, and without being able to take off their boots or get any rest, and being attacked every day by fresh troops.

In that short period, March 21st to 31st, the night of the 22nd will abide for ever in the minds of those who were privileged to live through it, for it was afterwards ascertained that the Battalion had helped to hold up at least three German divisions and had materially contributed to the successful crossing of the Somme by the 5th Army. The men of the 2/5th went into action at 5 a.m. on March 21st, and on the 23rd, at 3.30 a.m., they had only withdrawn two miles from their original position in the Battle Zone ; in the meantime they had been attacked continuously for nearly forty-eight hours by three German divisions. If the Battalion had done nothing else in the war, this episode alone would have earned for it a niche in the Nation's Valhalla. Capt. Howitt, the Brigade Major, in a letter to Brig.-Gen. White, describes the period as one long continuous battle and trek. He goes on to compute the Brigade casualties at about 1,800 officers and men, the Glosters quota being 20 officers and 550 other ranks. These figures testify to the grimness of the struggle.

Notes by Brig.-Gen. R. White (184th Brigade) include these passages :

" The 2/5th Gloucester Battalion was in the Battle Zone on March 21st and was the last to withdraw, having been ordered to cover the withdrawal of the 184th Brigade, which was itself acting as rearguard to the 61st Division and 18th Corps. During the day the enemy made no impression on the Battle Zone. The Glosters arrived as a rearguard in front of Beauvois at about 4 p.m. on the 22nd and 'stuck it' till 3.30 a.m. on the 23rd, all other troops having retired at 10.30 p.m. on the 22nd."

Maj.-Gen. Sir Colin Mackenzie writing to Brig.-Gen. White, says :

" The Division has fought in a magnificent way and as you may have seen, have been specially mentioned, a distinction which I value more than anything else . . . it is extraordinarily severe on this Division and I do not believe any Division in France has been kept at it so continuously from the 21st March as the 61st. We have lost 8,000 officers and men since that date and have had no chance of reorganising or anything else."

In an extract from special order of the day issued by the General Officer Commanding 61st Division, dated 18/4/18, the following words occur :

" Since the commencement of the great battle, March 21st, the 61st Division has fought against no less than fourteen German Divisions . . . after nearly a month's fighting, the 61st Division has not only stood up against these great odds, but remains a fighting unit, a record of which it may well be proud."

Lt.-Gen. Sir Ivor Maxse commanding 18th Corps, writes in the same strain :

" The more one looks at the performance of the British Divisions concerned on March 21st and 22nd, the more one is struck by the reflection that they did well, wonderfully well, and would have held the battle line intact, if every Division had been on a 4,000 yards frontage on that date."

And to Gen. Sir Colin Mackenzie :

" Well done again, Sixty-one.—Maxse."

Yet again, Sir Hubert Gough, Commanding 5th Army, writes to the General Officer Commanding 61st Division :

" I want to thank you and your gallant Division for the great work you did in March with the 5th Army. No Division did better or even as well as yours and I said so in my report."

The " Narrative of Operations " issued by Gen. Sir Colin Mackenzie follows :—

OFFICIAL NARRATIVE OF OPERATIONS

CARRIED OUT BY THE 61ST DIVISION, FROM MARCH 21ST
TO APRIL 2ND, 1918, ON THE ARRAS–LA FERE FRONT

From the beginning of March it became increasingly evident that the enemy contemplated, either an attack, or a demonstration on a large scale, on the St. Quentin Front.

The chief factors tending to foreshadow this, in addition to the information obtained from prisoners, were the construction of new hospitals, sidings, aerodromes, and dumps, in the enemy's back areas, though in the forward areas little or no new work or movement of a suspicious nature had appeared until the 12th. About this date, air photographs revealed the presence of some 500 objects, about 15ft. by 5ft., grouped in various parts of the front between Bellenglise and St. Quentin, hidden from observation from the ground. These objects daily increased in number, until some 1,000 or more were visible by the 19th, and when fired on by our artillery were proved by explosions to be an extensive system of forward ammunition dumps.

Parties of the enemy were observed examining our lines with glasses and maps, and during the week before the offensive, forward pieces of artillery, brought to within 1,000 yards of our outpost line, carried out registration.

Throughout the whole period hostile artillery preserved a marked inactivity in spite of our raids and continual night bombardments.

The Headquarters of the 61st Division were at Auroir, and the Headquarters of the 18th Corps at Ham.

On the night of the 20th/21st of March a strong raid by the 2/6th Warwicks was made against the enemy trenches east of Fayet. This raid was completely successful, and resulted in the capture of fifteen prisoners and three machine-guns, establishing the fact that the enemy forces opposite our immediate front had been increased by at least two Divisions, and, from prisoners' statements, that an attack would be launched on the morning of the 21st.

21st. This enabled warning to be circulated to neighbouring Divisions and Corps, and the order " Man Battle Stations " was sent out at 4.43 a.m.

The Division was normally disposed with three Brigades in line, each with one Battalion in the *Forward Zone*, one in the *Battle Zone*, and one in reserve. 182nd Infantry Brigade was on the right, 184th Infantry Brigade was in the centre and 183rd Infantry Brigade on the left. Their resting Battalions were at Germaine, Ugny, and Beauvois respectively.

The Battalions of Brigades detailed to hold the Battle Zone defences and the rear defences of Holnon Wood were all in position by 7.15 a.m., and the Brigade in Corps Reserve (89th Infantry Brigade) in Beauvois by 9 a.m.

At 4.35 a.m. a heavy bombardment commenced all along the front, which was accompanied by severe gas shelling against redoubts and battery positions, though in the case of the latter, fire effect was in many cases neutralised owing to the construction and occupation of alternative positions.

The hostile bombardment continued with varying intensity throughout the day—the principal feature being intense area shoots destroying or rendering untenable by gas all Brigade Headquarter huts, and dugouts, as far back as to include the Battle Zone.

During the early hours of the morning a heavy mist had set in, under cover of which hostile infantry advanced to the assault at approximately 9.30 a.m. and were enabled to press forward to within a few yards of our posts and overwhelm them before any target was visible.

By 11 a.m. it became evident that the line of resistance had been penetrated at several points, and by noon the enemy was reported to have surrounded all three redoubts in the Forward Zone and to be working his way towards the Battle Zone, making use of valleys and depressions in the ground.

These Redoubts in the Forward Zone—held by the 5th Gordons, 4th Oxfords, and 8th Worcesters, fought with splendid gallantry throughout the day, and were still holding out at 4.10 p.m. when the buried cable—which had up to this hour remained intact, ceased to operate. The last message received was from Lieut. Cunningham, 4th Oxford and Bucks, who was then the senior Officer Commanding in Enghien Redoubt, asking permission for the garrison to try and cut their way out. This permission was given, and also, by Corps Instructions, to the other Redoubts at the same time. Except for a few odd men that came in during the night, none returned from the Battalions fighting in the Forward Zone.

By mid-day the enemy had penetrated the Battle Zone of the 24th Division on our left, and after occupying Maissemy was preparing to advance against Villecholes Hill from that direction. With the exception of the line of the 183rd Infantry Brigade on the extreme left, held by the Argyll and Sutherland Highlanders, which had been forced to take up a defensive flank facing north through Mill Hill, the enemy had nowhere reached our Battle Zone at this hour.

At 1.40 p.m. the first of many attacks against Mill Hill developed from the direction of Maissemy, and at 6.10 p.m. the 4th Royal Berks, moving from Marteville, their left on Mill Hill, counter-attacked with the object of recovering the whole of the Battle Zone positions on the high ground south of Maissemy, in order to enable the 24th Division to counter-attack against the village itself. This attack held the enemy for the time, but was only partially successful, the Commanding Officer having been killed during the early stages.

At about 10 p.m. the battle quietened down. The enemy had suffered serious losses, not only from the Redoubts in the Forward Zone, but also from rifle and machine-gun fire from the Battle Zone and Mill Hill, machine-guns being particularly effective from a position south of Attilly towards

Savy Wood, and a position on the Maison de Garde–Holnon road.

Except on our left, as already described, the enemy was unable to make good any ground in our Battle Zone. Nine guns, belonging to two 18-pounder batteries between Maissemy and Villecholles, which had been over-run, were fought for and recovered on the morning of the 22nd, and a forward section of a Battery east of Maison de Garde killed a large number of the enemy, firing over open sights.

Considerable difficulty was experienced throughout the day in regulating the various pre-arranged schemes of barrage fire, owing to communication between Groups and Batteries being continually severed, whilst fire by observation, on the other hand, was quite impossible owing to the heavy ground mist.

22nd. Corps Headquarters closed at Ham at 9.47 a.m., reopening at Nesle at the same hour.

A heavy mist had again settled on the battle front during the night.

At 7.25 a.m. an intense barrage was put down on Mill Hill, and from 8 a.m. to 10 a.m. heavy attacks developed, which were repulsed by the stubborn defence of the Argyll and Sutherland Highlanders.

At 10.30 a.m. two Companies of the 4th Royal Berks again counter-attacked in this direction, cleared the ground, and remained—one Company east of Mill Hill in the position of the counter-attacking Company of the Battalion, and the other Company at Mill Hill itself.

The enemy did not succeed in any of his repeated efforts against our Battle Zone, but at 12.10 p.m. the Royal Scots had to be moved from the rear of Holnon Wood Defences towards Villeveque and the Omignon Valley, in order to guard the left flank, and to meet the threat against our left caused by a considerable number of the enemy advancing westwards on the north side of the Omignon.

Meanwhile strong attacks were being launched against

the left of the 30th Division on our right, though our right itself was not being severely pressed.

Owing to the situation on our left, the Corps, at 12.50 p.m., ordered the Division to withdraw to the Vaux–Villeveque line, keeping in touch with the 30th Division at Etreillers. This line consisted of a lately constructed system dug to an average depth of 18 inches, which, though wired, was traversed by numerous roads and tracks, where unfilled gaps existed.

The withdrawal was successfully accomplished by 5.40 p.m., each brigade being covered by its own artillery group, rear troops withdrawing first, and on reaching the Vaux–Villeveque line, halting and allowing successive lines to pass through.

Throughout this operation the enemy maintained a heavy pressure on our rearguard.

The division was now disposed on a frontage of approximately 5,000 yards, with a depth of 1,000 yards, and shortly after taking up positions was heavily attacked from the direction of Attilly—hostile artillery fire, directed by numerous low-flying aeroplanes, being particularly severe and accurate.

During the remainder of the day the enemy pressed his attacks with extreme violence against Beauvois and our junction with the 30th Division at Vaux, and by 7.45 p.m. had succeeded in forcing his way through the latter village, and was working his way along the valley into Germaine.

Hostile fire was so severe that movement in the neighbourhood of Beauvois was almost impossible, and this, combined with the ever-increasing pressure by fresh forces of the enemy against troops which had suffered heavily in two days' continuous fighting, greatly interfered with attempts at re-organisation.

To this fact the breaking of the rear line of defence on the right, late in the afternoon, was no doubt to a great extent due.

Divisional Headquarters had moved from Auroir to

Matigny at 2.45 p.m. and Corps Headquarters closed at Nesle, re-opening at Roye at 3.35 p.m.

At 7.50 p.m. orders were received from Corps for the Division to be relieved in the rear zone by the 59th Brigade, 20th Division. This was cancelled, and the 59th Brigade was ordered to take up the switch line Villers St. Christophe–Matigny, and to cover the withdrawal of the 61st Division across the Somme.

Divisional Headquarters moved to the cross-roads at I.22.d.1.3, west of Voyennes at 11 p.m.

This withdrawal across the Somme was accomplished by 6 a.m. 23rd, Brigades actually fighting a rearguard action, as the 20th Division were withdrawn according to orders at 1 a.m.

The 183rd Infantry Brigade did not leave its position until nearly midnight, and the 5th Glosters (184th Infantry Brigade) held on till 2.30 a.m. on 23rd, the Brigade Commander of the latter brigade having been wounded and the Brigade Major taken prisoner—though he subsequently effected his escape ; the receipt of orders was by these accidents delayed.

The surplus battalion, which consisted of the nucleus personnel left out of action in each battalion, had been ordered to proceed, half to Offoy and half to Voyennes, there to defend the bridge-heads until all the troops had passed through. These orders were gallantly carried out, the battalion subsequently coming under command of 182nd Infantry Brigade and taking part in the counter-attack against Ham on the 24th.

During the afternoon of the 22nd the 61st Division Artillery passed to the command of the 20th Division and the Infantry Brigades to the command of the same division on the 23rd. It should be here stated that the artillery of the 61st Division ceased to take part in the operations carried out by the Division after the 24th, being drawn southwards, and subsequently co-operating with the French in that area.

On the morning of the 23rd the Division, with a fighting strength of approximately 600 per Brigade, was disposed as follows west of the River Somme :—

Division Headquarters at Rethonvillers.

182nd Infantry Brigade under 20th Division in and north of Hombleux, and detailed for defences of the Somme near Canizy, owing to the fact that the 60th Brigade had been unable to withdraw across the river.

183rd and 184th Infantry Brigades concentrated at Nesle and Languevoisin–Billancourt respectively.

2 Companies of the 1/5th D.C.L.I. (pioneers) and 200 surplus details in post covering bridge at Offoy.

3 Field Companies R.E. under G.O.C. 183rd Infantry Brigade for the defences of Nesle.

By 6 p.m. all three brigades were placed under command of 20th Division and from this hour onwards until the night of the 25th troops of the division fought in different areas under two different divisions, elements of the 182nd Infantry Brigade, consisting of the 1/5th D.C.L.I. and surplus battalion, being transferred to the 30th Division at midnight on the 23rd/24th.

Owing to the fact that subsequent operations carried out by the Brigades of the Division took place in widely separated theatres until the 26th the narrative of each must be dealt with in turn.

The 182nd Infantry Brigade at noon on 23rd carried out a counter-attack against Ham station, and after successfully reaching the railway, were held up by machine-gun fire both from the station and north of the Somme.

On the 24th the pioneer Battalion and 200 of the surplus Battalion made a successful counter-attack, which carried them close up to Ham. Both of these attacks, though costly, succeeded effectively in delaying the enemy advance.

The subsequent withdrawal of the 182nd Infantry Brigade and the pioneers was carried out in conjunction with the

French to area Hangest-en-Santerre–Le Quesnel, when, during the night of the 25th, they returned to command of the 61st Division.

The 183rd Infantry Brigade were ordered, on the morning of the 24th, to counter-attack and re-establish the line on the canal bank, the enemy during the night having forced a crossing to Bethencourt. One battery of Canadian motor machine-guns was placed at disposal of General Officer Commanding 183rd Infantry Brigade for this purpose.

The attack, which was launched from assembled positions east and south of Mesnil St. Nicaise, succeeded at first in driving the enemy into Bethencourt but later, advancing in large numbers, the enemy forced our troops back on to the Morchain–Rouy Le Grand road.

Throughout this operation our left flank remained entirely in the air.

The Brigade was then withdrawn to banks and trenches half a mile south of Mesnil St. Nicaise, and later in the evening was ordered to take up a line from Mesnil towards Potte, placing a detachment in Potte to gain touch with the 8th Division whose right was supposed to rest north of the village, in order to conform to the withdrawal of the 20th Division to the Noyon–Nesle Canal line.

Mesnil St. Nicaise was taken by the enemy before this order could be carried out, and a line was formed running west of the village to Potte.

On the morning of the 25th a general attack developed along the whole front, in which a number of Argyll and Sutherland Highlanders were cut off south of Mesnil. This attack was held up from the Chaulnes–Nesle Railway, with the help of the Canadian Motor Machine-Gun Brigade, for over 3 hours, until all ammunition had been expended.

A line was then taken up north-west of Billancourt Village in conjunction with the French, who were at that time digging in along the Billancourt–Herly road, whilst one battalion of the brigade (9th Royal Scots) withdrew in the direction of Fonches and occupied a position under orders of General Officer Commanding 72nd Infantry Brigade.

That night the Brigade was withdrawn to Le Quesnel, and came under command of 61st Division.

The 184th Infantry Brigade were moved to positions about Hombleux at noon on the 24th, to be ready to counter-attack towards either Canizy, Offoy, or Voyennes, and later in the day, owing to the increasing pressure of the enemy forcing the left of the 30th Division, were ordered to take up a line between Quiquerry and Bacquencourt bridges to conform to the withdrawal of the 20th Division on to the line Noyon–Nesle Canal.

This line was held until the afternoon of the 25th, when the brigade reverted to the command of the 61st Division after withdrawing to the Hangest-en-Santerre–Le Quesnel area.

Division Headquarters had moved to Parvillers at 2.45 p.m. on the 24th, and to Beaucourt-en-Santerre at 10 p.m. on the 25th.

Headquarters of the 18th Corps were now at Moreuil.

The night of the 25th passed without incident, the three Brigades of the Division being no longer in contact with the enemy.

At noon on the 26th all available forces of the Division were ordered by Corps to block the Roye–Amiens road against the enemy, who were reported to be advancing in force.

A line was taken up from Beaucourt to Mezieres, and during the night the brigades moved forward to Le Quesnel and Hangest in support of the 20th Division and 30th Division, where they remained throughout the 27th, dispositions of the units being frequently changed to meet the tactical situation.

At 8.10 p.m. on 27th March the Division was withdrawn from Le Quesnel and embussed for Villers Bretonneux, after relief by the 133rd French Division, and passed to the command of the 19th Corps, whose advanced Headquarters were at that town. Division Headquarters opened at Villers Bretonneux at 11.15 p.m.

At midnight orders were given for an attack to be made against Lamotte at dawn on the 28th ; consequently, the buses carrying the infantry were deflected at Aubercourt and taken to Marcelcave, where troops debussed.

This operation, however, was eventually postponed at 3 a.m. on representations being made to the Corps that no previous reconnaissance had been possible, that the necessary troops had not yet arrived, and that all were in an exhausted condition.

The Division was therefore disposed along the railway running east and west at Marcelcave, with one Brigade in reserve in the village itself, ready to attack should the enemy advance west from Lamotte.

At 11 a.m. on the 28th the 183rd and 184th Infantry Brigades attacked the village of Lamotte, after orders had been received from the Corps for this operation to take place at once, Corps also stating that there were very few enemy in the village and that the attack must take place without artillery support.

The attack went well on the right, where one Company pushed up to the outskirts of Lamotte and held on for some six hours, until driven out, having suffered heavy casualties by shell fire and machine-guns from Bayonvillers, which fire such artillery as had become available was unable to keep down.

On the left the attack was held up by machine-gun fire from Warfusee Abancourt, and efforts to work one Company round the north-west side of this village failed.

Throughout the operation enemy shelling was very heavy on Marcelcave and the railway cutting running east from the village, whilst enemy field guns fired over open sights at our attacking troops.

At 3.40 p.m. the Corps ordered the withdrawal of the two Brigades from in front of Lamotte, and by nightfall the Division was disposed on the following line :—

182nd Infantry Brigade covering the eastern face of Marcelcave ; 184th Infantry Brigade in the railway cutting facing north ; 183rd Infantry Brigade about one mile west of Marcelcave on a line due south from the railway.

During the night the enemy attacked the village from the south-east, the nucleus garrisons and the 39th Division who should have continued the line on the right of the 182nd Infantry Brigade having apparently withdrawn soon after dark.

The enemy had obtained possession of Marcelcave by dawn, and our line was established clear of the south-western outskirts of the village, running due north to a point about $\frac{1}{4}$ mile south of the main Amiens–St. Quentin road in touch with troops of an American Labour Unit and other elements known as Carey's Force ; the 66th and 39th Divisions continued the line on our right.

29th. At 7 a.m. an order was received from the 19th Corps, which gave the general line to be held as Mezieres–Demuin–Marcelcave–Hamel, the 61st Division being placed in reserve on the right centre, specially detailed with the safeguarding of Marcelcave.

Marcelcave, as already stated, was no longer held by us when this message was received, our troops being actually engaged in preventing attempts by the enemy to debouch from the village.

At 5 p.m. advance Divisional Headquarters moved to Gentelles and rear Headquarters to Boves.

During the afternoon the 19th Corps stated that a line was being constructed running from the River Luce about Berthaucourt–Gentelles–Bois de Blangy to the River Somme, and that 2,000 troops of the 18th Division would be disposed on this line on arrival, from Gentelles to Villers Bretonneux–Amiens road under the command of the 61st Division. These troops arrived at Gentelles at midnight, and in consequence of an earlier report being received that the enemy had made headway north of Mezieres were ordered to occupy with nucleus garrisons a line from the southern edge of the Bois de Blangy to the Mezieres–Longueau road. Command of this line subsequently reverted to General Officer Commanding 18th Division at noon on the 30th.

The 9th Brigade (3rd Australian Division) were that night (29th) placed under the command of the Division to be used for counter-attack should the enemy advance westwards of either Gentelles or Villers Bretonneux, and the following morning a detachment of 4 cars of the Canadian Armoured Motor Machine-Gun Corps arrived at Gentelles and were placed under our orders for reconnaissance. These latter afterwards rendered invaluable assistance, both in obtaining speedy information at close contact with the enemy where no other means of doing so were available, and by their bold handling and enterprise inspired all ranks to further effort.

30th. On the morning of the 30th a counter-attack against Aubercourt by the 66th Division failed, and the consequent withdrawal to dig in on a line running north from Hangard apparently was the cause for a general tendency for troops further north to commence dribbling back in small parties, though no hostile pressure was reported against the line. This movement reached the 182nd Infantry Brigade south-west of Marcelcave, and their right flank was defused to meet the situation, officers being sent out to check any further withdrawal.

About 10 a.m. the Battalion astride the railway northeast of the village was entirely shelled out of its positions, and hostile artillery fire now became severe on the area south of this point.

Owing to the fact that the situation on our right was becoming increasingly serious, added to which the enemy could be seen thickening his line north of Aubercourt, orders were given to the 9th Australian Brigade to counter-attack, with the object of restoring the line from the east of Marcelcave to Aubercourt. Up to this time there had been practically no liaison obtainable with any artillery, though representations on the subject had been made to 19th Corps, both on the 29th and 30th ; it was therefore decided that the attack should be carried through without artillery support.

The operation was ably carried out by the 33rd Battalion, with the 34th in support, whilst the 12th Lancers (2nd Cavalry Division) worked in conjunction and protected the flanks. The attack reached and advanced from the wood east of the Bois de Hangard at 4.30 p.m. A few of the enemy had already penetrated the wood previous to this, threatening the right of the line held by us, but a Company of the 9th Royal Scots (183rd Infantry Brigade) advancing from the east corner of the wood, though suffering heavy casualties, maintained their ground until the counter-attack passed through.

The 12th Lancers, with one squadron on the left and the Scots Greys on the right, materially assisted in the success of the operation, apart from the moral support rendered by their splendid discipline under heavy shell fire.

Mention should also be made here of the excellent work done by the Horse Artillery Batteries, and the confidence which their bold handling instilled into all ranks whilst the cavalry were fighting with us.

This attack, though it did not reach its objectives, owing to artillery and strong opposition from the enemy, who were well entrenched and in force, succeeded, however, in restoring the line opposite the 39th and 66th Divisions.

On the night of the 30th, under orders received direct from 5th Army, the troops of the 61st Division, and the Australian Battalions who had taken part in the above operations, were relieved by the 35th Australian Battalion, and the 18th Division respectively, and the Division concentrated in Gentelles.

31st. During the morning of the 31st, the 182nd Infantry Brigade reported the 2/7th Warwicks and other elements attached had not been relieved by the Australian Brigade and these, together with 3 squadrons of the 2nd Cavalry

Division also in the line, south of the Villers Bretonneux–
Warfusee road, were ordered to be relieved the following
night.

April 1st. The 61st Division occupied the Berthaucourt–
Gentelles defences from the Bois l'Abbe to the Amiens–
Domart road, which line was improved and wired, until
the Division was withdrawn on the night of the 2nd to
Longueau, leaving behind a composite Company of machine-
guns under the orders of the 18th Division. This composite Company rejoined the Division on the 8th.

The casualties during this period amounted to :—272
Officers, 5,661 Other ranks.

(*Signed*)

Major-General,

28th May, 1918.   Commanding 61st Division.

CHAPTER X

FROM APRIL TO JUNE 24TH, 1918

THE 184th Brigade had withdrawn to Gentelles, just behind the line, and on April 3rd marched to Amiens, whence, after a wait of two hours, it proceeded for eight or ten miles in lorries, then marching another seven miles to the neighbourhood of Tailly. The 2/5th Glosters were billetted in Warlus.

While the Battalion was at this village, Major Christie Miller reported for duty as second in command on April 7th. The Battalion at the time consisted of Battalion Headquarters, six Company Officers and about 150 men. Lt.-Col. A. B. Lawson was in command and had just been awarded a well-merited D.S.O. ; Capt. Gray was still available as Adjutant, and Capt. Tomlins as Quartermaster. The strength of the Battalion was made up to respectable figures from various sources, and it soon became evident that it would quickly train up to the high standard it had attained before the retreat. Nevertheless, it was not an easy problem to absorb cooks, shoemakers, tailors, postmen, messmen, and transport men, most of whom had not done a day's company duty for three years. The mass of work lying ahead seemed prodigious ; much of the men's kits had been burnt at Attilly and the loss of fighting equipment had been enormous, but the speed with which Ordnance replenished these shortages deserves the highest praise.

There were all the usual problems to straighten out ; officers' Mess Accounts had been in the hands of officers who were killed or missing ; conduct sheets had been burnt ; the Canteen Corporal was missing ; officers' kits had been burnt ; money which had been drawn to pay the troops had been burnt.

Fortunately the Battalion had a strong administrative staff ; the orderly room was most efficient under Sgt. Gurney and Cpl. Allen ; then the Quartermaster did everything possible for the comfort of the troops, and the enterprise always displayed by Sgt. Gibbs was invaluable ; Sgt. Cater too and his pioneers did for the Battalion a volume of work which would have secured their instant expulsion from many a Union, and the way in which they " acquired " various useful material proved clearly that the Eighth Commandment had no place in their religious make-up.

Of the training staff, R.S.M. Spragg was still with the unit. Unlike many R.S.M.'s, whose usefulness is mainly confined to the " square," Sgt.-Major Spragg, besides being a first-class drill instructor, could instruct N.C.O.'s in field work, administration and routine duty. More important perhaps was the fact that he entered into the social and athletic side of the men's lives, and although a firm disciplinarian, he treated them with a consideration seldom shown by an R.S.M.

Much could be said in praise of the Lewis Gun training under Sgt. Davies, of the signallers under Sgt. Child, and of other departments of the Battalion, but since all were so well served and so willing to give of their best it is invidious to individualise.

Brig.-Gen. the Hon. R. White, C.B., had been wounded at Beauvois and his place had now been taken by Brig.-Gen. A. W. Pagan, D.S.O., of the Gloucester Regiment. The latter was a born fighter with the heart of a lion. He seemed to have two absorbing interests in life—the Gloucester Regiment and Rugby Football, so it is not to be wondered at that he won the approval of all ranks of the Battalion at once.

It had been intended that the 61st Division should rest

and reorganise in a comfortable part of the line, but an unexpected German break through on the Laventie front upset these calculations. News trickled through that the enemy had taken Laventie and that their progress was unchecked. It was obvious, therefore, that before very long the 2/5th would be in the fray again.

On the 12th the Battalion detrained at Steenbecque after a most unpleasant journey, and from then onwards, instead of resting, reorganising and training, as was hoped, the 184th Brigade was destined to remain in the line until June 24th.

The incessant roar of artillery in the direction of Bethune gave evidence of unwelcome activity. The Brigade was immediately pushed into the line in the neighbourhood of Robecq, the Glosters being in reserve at St. Venant.

The enemy attacked on April 13th, but were met and stopped on the line of the parallel streams of the Noc and the Clarence, between the villages of Calonne and Robecq. The morning mist which covered the attack cleared later in the day and it was then found that the enemy had brought up a light field gun on the Battalion's left and had abandoned it. A satisfactory feature of this attack was that it was driven off by infantry alone and largely by rifle fire from small isolated posts. This had a very stimulating effect on the newly joined drafts.

Late on the night 13th/14th the Battalion moved into billets at St. Venant. As far as possible the billets were fixed up in cellars and the necessity for this precaution soon became apparent as a 4.2 shell burst on the roof of a house just opposite to Battalion Headquarters.

St. Venant was not as delightful a spot as when the Battalion first passed through it in 1916, for the tide of war had now rolled almost to its outskirts and it was being steadily pounded to bits. It yielded, however, a great deal of material that gave joy to the soldier's heart : there was, for instance, a complete store of almost every form of military equipment, and so, many of the Battalion's urgent needs were satisfied. There was, moreover, hardly a cellar

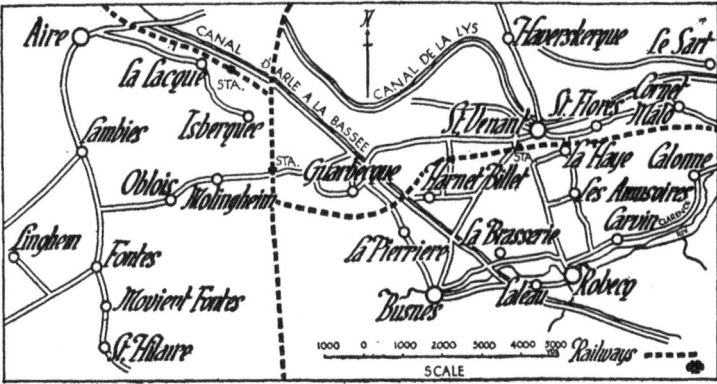

The St. Venant Area.

that was not well stocked with vintage as well as commoner wines and it says much for the troops that, with free access to these amenities, there was not a single case of indiscipline.

On April 16th the Battalion left these hospitable quarters and went into the line.

The line consisted of small isolated groups, those by the river being of the hip bath variety and it was held by all four companies.

The country around had been left by its inhabitants well stocked, and here at any rate starvation was not one of the hardships of war. With a diet of roast chicken, fresh eggs, vegetables and an adequate supply of claret, it is no surprise that for the moment rations were of no account. A retreat had indeed its compensations.

The enemy kept up continuous attempts at infiltration. Bacquerolles Farm, for instance, had changed hands a number of times, and was at the moment held by the Glosters.

On the night of April 17th/18th a very fine effort by a platoon of the 2/5th prevented what might have been a disastrous break through. The Germans reoccupied the Farm and a counter-attack was ordered. This was carried out under Sgt. White of A Company. The operation was a brilliant little affair and was completely successful. Sgt. White and his platoon numbered under twenty men, but the party captured the Farm and completely restored the situation. Seventeen prisoners were taken as well as a machine-gun and over twenty Germans were left dead on the ground.

Sgt. White was awarded the D.C.M. for the effort and few decorations have been better earned. The captured machine-gun was afterwards presented to the City of Gloucester.

The lighter side of warfare was provided by a cattle drive organised by the Commanding Officer on the morning of the 19th. A motley herd of beasts was rounded up and driven up to Headquarters, but while orders as to their

SERGT. E. G. WHITE, D.C.M.

MAJOR G. L. DAY (CENTRE), O.C. COMPANY, WITH OFFICERS OF B COMPANY,
GAPENNES, JANUARY, 1917.

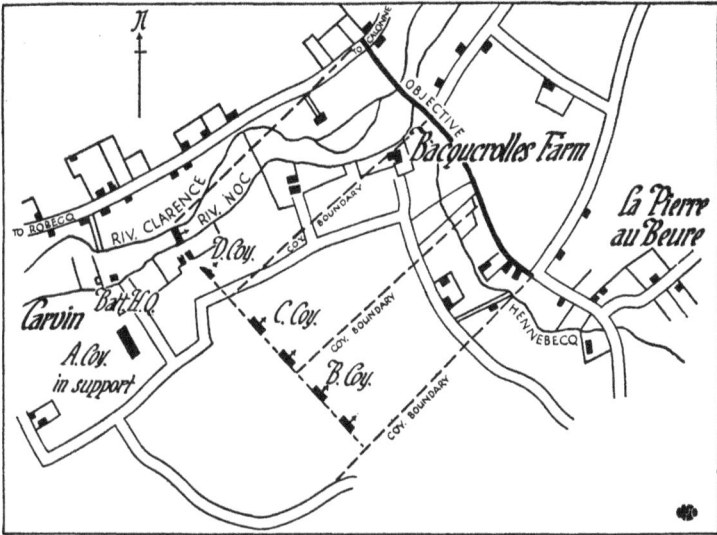

Attack on
Bacquerolles Farm.

disposal were being argued out they began to streak back for home and had to be rounded up again.

On April 23rd the Battalion again distinguished itself. At Bacquerolles Farm, and to the south-east of it, the British line formed a re-entrant. The object of the attack was to straighten out this line. One Battalion from each Brigade in the Division was employed, and from the 184th Brigade the 2/5th Glosters was the selected Battalion.

The attack commenced at 4.30 a.m. and, so far as the Glosters were concerned, it was completely successful. The artillery barrage did its work so well that the enemy was badly demoralised before the infantry came to grips. Setting off from a line taped out by Major Christie Miller and Capt. John Hunter, the Glosters gained all their objectives and consolidated, capturing 79 prisoners and 10 machine-guns.

At noon the Germans opened a heavy bombardment on the Battalion's new position and continued the shelling till 5 a.m. on the 27th when they landed their counter-attack, but their troops had not a great deal of fight left in them after their hammering on the previous day. The counter-attack was thus easily beaten off and over sixty prisoners were brought in.

The casualties of the Battalion were considerable, nearly 100 having been suffered during the bombardment. The losses included 3 officers and 28 other ranks killed, 21 missing, 1 officer and 100 other ranks wounded ; the wounded including C.S.M. Parsons. It was, however, a first-rate action, ably carried out and led by Lt.-Col. Lawson, who got a bullet through his tin hat during the course of the proceedings. Great satisfaction was felt by all ranks when the Commanding Officer was awarded a bar to his D.S.O. for this operation. A great deal of the success was due to the Brigade Signalling Officer, who, in defiance of all regulations, laid a ladder line which resisted the heavy bombardment and kept communication intact. On April 27th, the 61st Division was unlucky, as Major-Gen. Sir Colin

Mackenzie was wounded. The Division thus lost the service of an able leader who had been with it since February 1916. In the birthday honours in the following June he was gazetted K.C.B., an honour which he had so well earned and one which redounded to the credit of the Division which he had served with such distinction. His post was filled by Major-Gen. F. J. Duncan, Royal Scots, who retained command of the Division till the Armistice. At this time, Captain Dudbridge was awarded a bar to his M.C., and Captain Gray was awarded the M.C.

Captain Dudbridge ("Dudders," as he was affectionately called by his brother officers) came out with the Battalion in 1916. He had shown his resource and efficiency throughout the Battalion's most critical days. He possessed, too, a genial and hearty manner which immediately invited friendship. He was a very fine rugby forward, a qualification which never fails to rouse the admiration of a West Countryman, and he had an amazing capacity for telling yarns and for making a very good story out of an insignificant incident.

Captain Gray was of a different calibre; punctilious in every duty connected with his office, unobtrusive and apt to under-estimate his abilities. He did remarkably fine work on March 21st and 22nd, and was always loyal and efficient where both persons and causes were concerned. He was universally respected and probably had his friends among those who knew him best.

Both of these officers well merited the above distinctions, and the announcement of the awards was received with great satisfaction by the Battalion.

After three or four nights at Laleau, the Glosters moved into the Asylum at St. Venant, from which the Assistant Provost Marshal had recently removed the inmates. The conditions under which they lived there might have been very much worse. Somehow or other, through the ministrations of the Sergeant Cook and ten francs, a pianoforte was borrowed for the Sergeants' Mess. A piano on active service may sound an unnecessary and rather futile luxury, but as a matter of fact it is an asset of great value, because it provides constant entertainment for both officers and men, and not least, is considered indispensable by the Chaplain for the Sunday services.

There followed four days in the old line, then four in support round La Brasserie, where some casualties were suffered from artillery fire ; then four more at the Asylum, and lastly, four in the line, commencing on May 14.

About this time the Brigade line was reorganised so as to admit of two battalions in the line, the one in front of Robecq with Headquarters at Carvin, the other carrying on the line towards St. Floris, with Headquarters at Les Amusoires. The turns in the line were of eight days' duration, alternating with four days in Brigade Reserve at La Pier iere, a pleasant village still intact and situated a mile and a half west of Busnes.

During all this time considerable shelling went on, and it was of that promiscuous variety which is so much more unpleasant than a definite strafe on a definite area. The enemy, however, got far more than he gave and the stream of our shells passing overhead was everlasting by day and night : if it stopped, one missed something at once and imagined that something had gone wrong with the works. The result of the British shelling was made apparent later on when the advance began and it was found that the cemeteries, which had been in German hands, were packed with back-area casualties.

An amusing incident, reminiscent of a sheriff's officer distraining for debt, occurred at La Pierriere. Furniture had been acquired from Robecq for the Sergeants' Mess, and this had been handed over to the next unit as a matter of course. However, a Frenchman arrived with a card and an order from the Assistant Provost Marshal authorising him to remove the furniture. The house was therefore again furnished from Robecq, but again the Frenchman arrived with his card and order. For the third time the house was

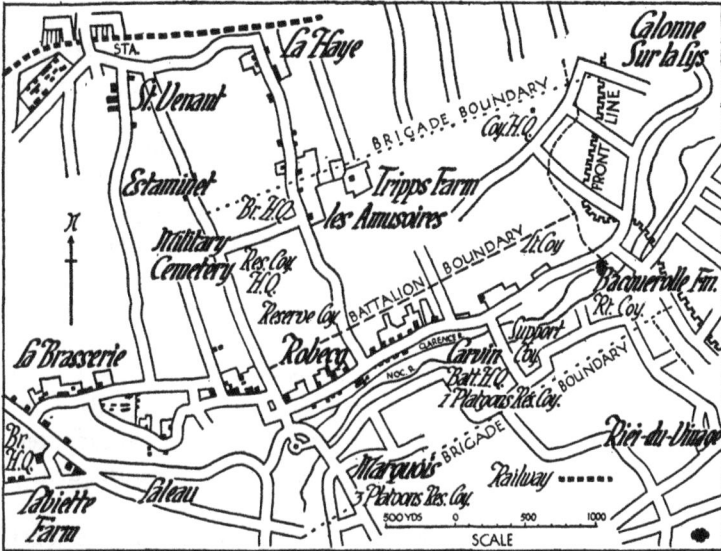

Right Brigade Front :
Robecq–Carvin Line.

refurnished and for a third time the Frenchman arrived with his card and order—but this time he found representatives of the original units waiting to receive him. He was sent under escort to the Assistant Provost Marshal and the furniture was retained.

During the summer months the influenza epidemic began to assert itself, and in addition to this, the further difficulty had to be met of finding sufficient troops to hold the line.

On June 6th Major J. P. McMahon, a regular officer from the Gloucester Regiment, reported for duty. His services were of great value in several directions, but his usefulness was terminated abruptly, when a month later, at the Regimental Sports, an inconsiderate mule kicked him in the mouth, smashed his jaw and fractured his skull.

A six weeks rest was now promised. It was anticipated that this would be at Guarbecque, but it subsequently materialised at a place called Linghem.

Great preparations were made for the event : cricket gear was obtained from England ; a concert party was organised ; new clothing was indented for profusely ; canteen stores including an adequate supply of the soldier's nectar—beer—were provided and the Sergeant Cook made elaborate plans for feeding the troops. On the training side every form of activity had begun to take shape, and there were indications that there was going to be, what Col. Muir so aptly described, an " intensive rest."

Alas ! before these anticipations could be realised, the Battalion was plunged into gloom by the death of its Commanding Officer, Lt.-Col. A. B. Lawson, D.S.O., on June 24th, the morning before the final relief took place.

Lt.-Col. Lawson was walking, according to a dangerous habit which he had, in front of his line on the south side of the Noc stream and close to its banks : he had gone out alone to satisfy himself personally as to certain enemy dispositions, so that he might be able to pass on definite information to the relieving battalion, such was his conception of duty. He was seen a few yards from a German

LT.-COL. A. B. LAWSON, D.S.O. AND BAR.
Commanding Officer, March 1918—June 1918.

post and then disappeared behind a hedge. The sound
of rifle shots and bombs was heard and he was not seen
again. His body was found some days later by a patrol
of the Worcesters, and was buried close to the Noc. The
grave was fenced in by the Battalion and a cross erected.
Of him, one of his officers wrote :

"He was a most wonderful personality and as one
knew him better, admiration grew into affection. He
was the ablest soldier of his day . . . tall, good-looking,
a fine athlete and a magnificent horseman."

Brig.-Gen. Pagan wrote of him :

"This officer was only approached by one other as a
battalion commander among the many I met in France.
He was absolutely fearless, very able, and was devoted
to the welfare of his men. He was always unruffled,
whatever the circumstances, and was a very fine leader
of men."

During the three months he had commanded the Battalion
he had acquired a complete grasp of every detail of regimental life. He had a wonderful gift of dropping on weak
spots and by some masterly touch remedying them. He
possessed the advantages of staff and regimental training
so evenly balanced that it would be hard to say for which
his talents were best fitted.

His death was a great loss to the Army ; to the 11th
Hussars it was a very deep blow indeed : to the 2/5th Glosters
it was like a personal bereavement.

The command of the Battalion was temporarily taken over
by Major Christie Miller, M.C., an appointment which
was confirmed on July 11th.

CHAPTER XI

FROM JUNE 25TH TO OCTOBER 5TH, 1918

THE Battalion was relieved on June 25th and remained out of the line till August 5th.

On coming out of the line it bivouaced in the park at Busnes until daylight and then proceeded in buses to Linghem, a pretty village four and a half miles south-west of Aire. The weather was for the most part hot and training was carried out under difficult conditions.

Two features make Linghem memorable. One was the attack of Spanish influenza which affected the 184th Brigade. It started with the Oxfords and reached the Glosters about June 27th. Its ravages were so severe that within a fortnight 250 men went to hospital. The Army called it " P.U.O.", which stands for " pyrexia of unknown origin." Soldiers, both high and low, are very fond of denoting persons and things by capital letters. N.B.G., for instance, is a favoured combination of theirs, and indeed, would not under the circumstances have been an unsuitable substitute for P.U.O.

The other feature was that, though the Battalion was in rest some miles behind the line, the reality of war was kept in the foreground by the arrival each night of a column of motor buses sufficient to take the reserve battalion back to the line in case of an attack, so solicitous was the Higher Command that the Glosters should not miss any part of the show.

Capt. G. F. Davies, B Company's Commander in the old days, and who was at this time on the Instructional

Staff, was posted to the Battalion on July 1st for temporary duty.

On July 17th the Battalion made a further move to St. Hilaire. The march thither was one of those glorious muddles that annoy Staff Officers so much and mildly amuse those who take part in them. The arrival of the incoming units had been timed to coincide with the assembly of the outgoing ones, and the result of four units with transport crossing each other's line of march can be better imagined than described.

That there was a complete absence of training ground at St. Hilaire mattered little, as an unexpected move to Cohem was made on the 19th which involved an eight-mile trek in extreme heat.

" Rest " on active service is a fickle and overworked word, and on July 22nd a further move was made to Pont Asquin, in the 2nd Army area. This brought the 184th Brigade into touch with Gen. Sir Herbert Plumer, who inspected it on July 25th.

The Glosters and Berks were crowded into a low-lying meadow, and given a short ration of tents and trench shelters. Owing to wet weather the field became water-logged, but this discomfort was philosophically faced by sending for the regimental piano, which was billetted on S.A.A. boxes in the open under a trench shelter and appeared to confound the experts who prophesied its ruin.

A reconnaissance of the defensive line at La Kreule was made, and subsequently battalion commanders were taken to reconnoitre the forward areas in the neighbourhood of Meterem. This move to the 2nd Army was always a mystery outside the Higher Command. It has been stated that at this time there was a concentration on both sides on this front and that on a certain night both sides were standing to in expectation of being attacked. Again, it is known that a Canadian detachment was put into the line here until identified by the Germans, in order to deceive the latter as to the true point of the contemplated attack on August 8th on the Somme.   The fact that troops were ostentatiously marched up by day, put into conspicuous camps and marched back by night, leaving the camps standing, lends colour to this view.

The arrival of Capt. Lavender, who joined on July 24th and was posted to command C Company, was a great acquisition. He had come to visit the Brigadier under whom he had previously served, and by some unexplained means the Brigadier had managed to retain him and sent him to the Glosters.

On July 31st a return was made to St. Hilaire by night, where training was continued mostly on the roads until the move back to the forward area on August 4th. It was here that Major A. H. Huntington, D.S.O., Somerset Light Infantry, joined as second in command. He was a new Army officer who had come out with the 21st Division and had served with his battalion at Loos.

The above move, which was made by bus to Steenbecque, brought the Battalion to Arcadia Camp in Nieppe Forest, near the junction of the Canal de Nieppe and the Haze-brouck–St. Venant road.

This camp was not what its name implied : the huts were scattered among trees and were hard to find at night : they were in bad order, too : the roads were impassable for wheeled transport and the amenities were not improved by the presence of a battery of 8-inch guns immediately in front of the camp. A further trouble was the enthusiasm of the 5th Division, recently returned from Italy, for all things Italian. This misplaced zeal led to a crop of Italian place-names in the area which the troops could not pronounce and invariably confused.

The next night, August 8th, the Battalion took over the Arrewage line from the 12th Glosters—a relief uneventful except for the cordiality which characterised a relief by two battalions of the same regiment which had never before met. The line consisted of a line of disconnected posts running roughly from the Arrewage–Merville road bridge.

These posts were held by two Companies, each of which had two platoons and Company Headquarters in the support line. Battalion Headquarters was in a row of elephant dugouts at the junction of Forest-Candescure and Forest-les-Puresbecques roads, with a regimental aid post in an adjoining farm. Stores and rations were trollied up a light railway nearly to the support line.

The feature of this line was the Plate Becque, a muddy stream varying in width from 15 feet to 25 feet and of uncertain depth and with enemy posts along the opposite bank. There was a great deal of shelling over the line, especially at Candescure. A source of annoyance was the persistent shelling from a rear battery : the curious thing was that it included Battalion Headquarters, Machine-Gun Headquarters, Heavy Artillery Observation Post and two Company Headquarters in its line of fire. All complained vigorously and sent back compass bearings of the flash. It was positively asserted that there was no battery in this line and that it must be a German enfilading gun. One evening the Brigade Commander was nearly caught outside Battalion Headquarters. The search therefore started again : an energetic Royal Artillery liaison officer found a piece of one of the offending shells which was identified as a 60-pounder. The truant battery was then located and all was well.

During this tour the idea prevailed that the Germans had retired from the Plate Becque, as a Staff Officer had walked along the front line in broad daylight and had not been fired at. However, the Battalion patrols drew fire the same night, so it was, with some reason, assumed the German positions were still held.

On the night of August 9th the Northumberland Fusiliers were pushed through the Glosters to form a bridge-head crossing the Plate Becque. The attack failed, as the enemy were fully prepared and about 60 casualties were suffered. The Glosters were ordered to repeat the attack on the 11th. For this purpose eight bridges, 25 feet in length and light enough to be carried by two men, were requisitioned. On the day before the attack, Rennet Farm on the right, which was known to be held by machine-guns, and neighbouring farms, were unmercifully battered by artillery. The assault was to be carried out by D Company on the right and B on the left, each with four bridges, and was to commence at dawn.

The operation was entirely unsuccessful. Of the bridges, two were too short ; two broke, precipitating some Lewis gunners into the river, where their guns were lost ; the bridges, requiring six men to carry them, were observed ; the enemy was on the alert and brought the advancing troops under a merciless machine-gun fire, so that, although they succeeded in crossing the stream, little progress was made when the further bank was reached. The artillery barrage was inaccurate and ineffective, one heavy battery having mistaken Itchen Farm, which was inside the British lines, for an enemy position.

A small party of B Company under Sgt. Groves reached the road near Sniper's House, and a platoon of D Company under Lieut. London reached its objective : the first was overwhelmed and Sgt. Groves was killed ; the second, finding itself unsupported, withdrew under cover of the mist and smoke, and on its return journey surprised a German post and brought in a machine-gun and some prisoners. Lieut. London and five of his men were wounded, but all were safely got back. One section of D Company in the centre, under Corpl. Terrett, dug in beyond the river and held its ground until night, when it was attacked and driven back.

Corpl. Terrett received the D.C.M., and Ptes. Livings and Barrett were awarded the M.M.

Lieuts. Hucks and London were wounded, the Battalion casualties being 8 other ranks killed, 2 officers and 39 other ranks wounded, 3 other ranks wounded and missing.

Brig.-Gen. Pagan's comment on the operation is very much to the point :

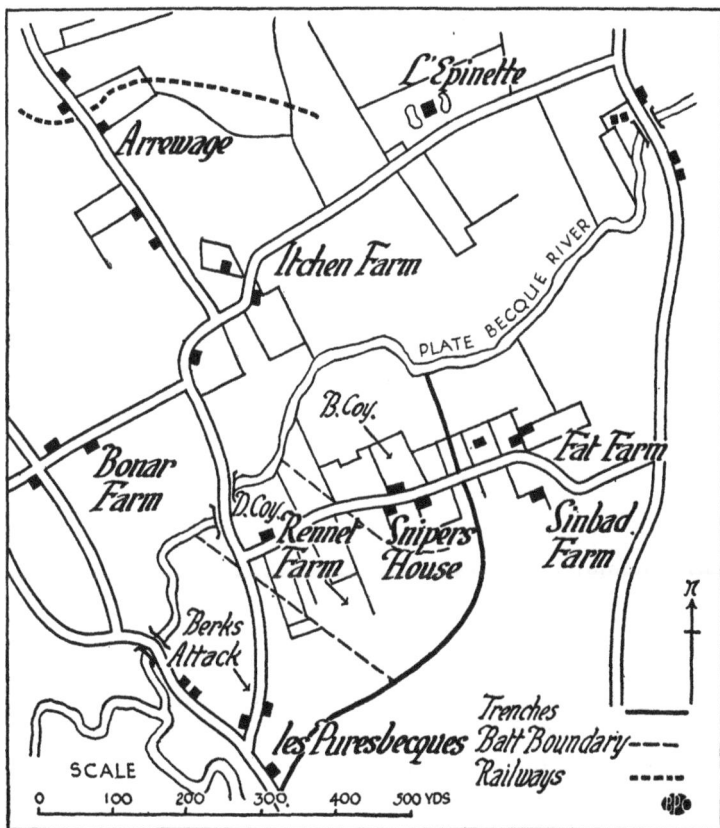

Attack on
Plate Becque.

1

" No doubt the operation was necessary, but there is also no doubt that it was impossible. For such an attack to have been successful it was necessary to have carried it out on a much wider front."

Having endured nine hard days the Battalion was relieved on August 14th and, after a march to Nieppe Forest on what the 5th Division insisted on calling Via Roma, entrained in small open trucks for La Lacque camp, which was reached at 4.30 a.m.

This was a most delightful hut camp, but it provided only scanty training ground. As, however, the rest only lasted a week, one day of which was spent in cleaning up, another in fitting gas respirators, while a third was a Sunday, this was of little consequence. The troops were always mildly amused at what they considered the waste of time and money spent in changing and fiddling with gas helmets. What they did not know was that when German prisoners were captured, specimens of their gas helmets were sent to England to be tested by the best chemists in order to find out against what new gas the British troops would have to be protected.

On August 21st an unexpected order was received to entrain at the camp station and move forward to Spresiano Camp in Nieppe Forest on one of the hottest days imaginable—a day on which candles, soap and butter merely disappeared because they had not the time to melt. Three days were spent here, one being occupied by an inspection by the General Officer Commanding, a somewhat explosive proceeding culminating in a vigorous and outspoken address on the qualities expected of a soldier. Large parties had to be found for agricultural duties, but it must be admitted that these duties were not carried out with the zeal usually associated with the Battalion.

On August 25th the Battalion moved forward in support round the Plate Becque. The position was roughly the objective of the attack on the 11th. The Oxfords held a line in the neighbourhood of Neuf Berquin and moved

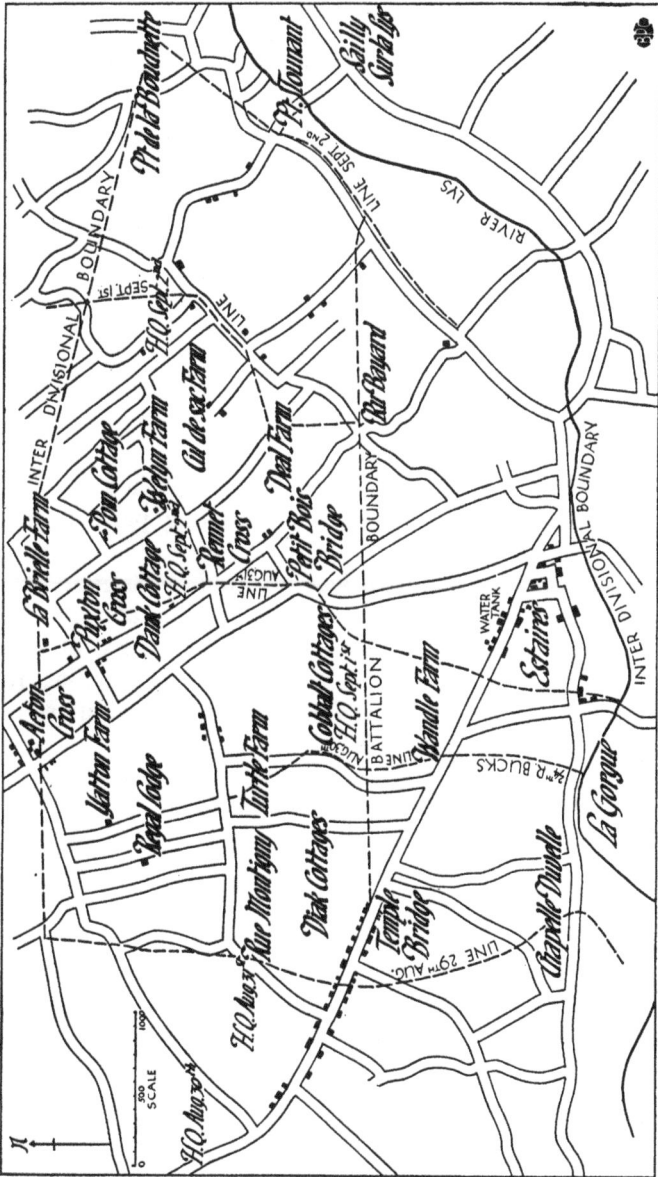

The Advance, August 29th to Sept. 2nd, 1918.

forward considerably in their four days' tour. The Glosters spent their four days fairly quietly, but the enclosures round Sniper's House, where the Headquarters of two companies stood, and Itchen Farm were heavily shelled. They relieved the Oxfords and one company of the 11th Camerons on August 29th/30th, taking over a line in front of Neuf Berquin. On the 31st the advance was pushed further forward to the line Meteren Becque–Puxton cross-roads.

On September 1st the advance continued, but difficulty was encountered by C Company in the centre and A Company on the left from enemy rearguards who held farm buildings with machine-guns and were well supported by artillery. By evening these difficulties had been overcome.

At dawn on the 2nd three companies pushed on and reached, unopposed, the main road running parallel and west of the Lys.

Later on in the morning it was reported by Brigade that the Berks had entered Sailly unopposed, but attempts to advance to the Lys soon proved the inaccuracy of this information. D Company came in for heavy shelling in the afternoon, when it moved forward to the support of B Company, then in the line.

Words give but a feeble impression of the strenuousness of these four days. With only a skeleton of Battalion Headquarters, an insufficiency of runners, an inadequate supply of wire, and a constantly moving line, there was the utmost difficulty in obtaining information from the line and transmitting it to Brigade. The whole tour provided a most useful initiation into the conduct of the moving battle after the long period of stationary warfare. During this tour the casualties had been heavy, numbering about 65.

On the night of September 2nd the Battalion was relieved by a battalion of the Warwicks. The relief was a most difficult one, as the advance continued until late and one company could not be located at the map reference given. However, the relieving company was despatched to the required position, and the missing company was left to find out for itself that it had been relieved since it was assumed that no body of men, possessing the soldier instinct, would remain in the line longer than was necessary.

A word is here due to Capt. Eric Harvey for the way in which he handled his company in this advance. His leadership was most inspiring ; there had been heavy fighting, and wherever the fighting was most severe, there was Harvey. He was awarded a bar to the M.C. for these operations, but alas ! he was not destined to wear it as he was killed on September 30th.

The relief on September 2nd was celebrated by the Germans with a brisk bombardment of Headquarters. The Battalion returned to the area from which it had started ; companies were given a map square apiece and told to find their own accommodation.

Two days later a move forward to the positions of September 2nd was made, the Warwicks having by now continued the advance. Stores were moved forward, necessary re-equipment was proceeded with and, still more necessary, baths of an amateur kind were instituted.

One interesting feature of the training was a scheme carried out over the country taken between August 29th and September 2nd, but the unreality of such practices was disclosed by the fact that the 6,000 yards which it had taken four days to wrest from the enemy rearguards was captured under these less exacting conditions in about three hours.

The next move was to the outskirts of Estaires. While here, the education experts descended upon the Battalion and expressed much dissatisfaction with the Battalion's neglect of its educational opportunities. Those who fought through these strenuous days are still puzzled to know how any man can be expected to study regimental history or write essays while he is continually on the move and continually running up against enemy rearguards : it was, and still is, physically, mentally and morally impossible.

Life in the reoccupied area was full of incident. For three weeks things blew up. In Estaires a house went sky-high nearly every day. A cross-road in the centre of the town blew up just after the Assistant Provost Marshal had passed, as also did a bit of road by the water point while the Oxfords' water cart was refilling : the horses were knocked over, but no damage was done. A farm between Montigny and Cobbalt Cottages went up seventeen days after the area had been reoccupied. The town of Merville had been completely wrecked ; no house possessed a second story and the streets had to be dug out like Pompeii.

While at Cobbalt Cottages orders were received on September 27th to carry out an attack immediately on returning to the line. The object of the army commander was to expedite the German retirement by attacking a key position on each divisional front. To the Glosters was assigned Junction Post.

Two days of strenuous organisation followed, including a practice attack over a course strongly resembling the features to be encountered.

On the night of the 29th the Battalion relieved the Oxfords, who were holding a line of posts more or less on the forming-up line and to do so proceeded through Estaires and up the same road traversed by the troops on the way up to the attack of July 19th, 1916.

It was a dark night and there was considerable difficulty in getting companies into their forming-up positions.

The plan was that C Company was to attack Junction Post and take up a position in front of it ; A Company was to take the enclosed ground on the left of it and connect with the Berks on the left ; D Company was to take an enemy trench on the right front and occupy it with four posts each holding a platoon ; B Company was to find two platoons to support D Company on the right flank and two in reserve behind Battalion Headquarters—Bat-

CAPT. E. H. HARVEY,
M.C. AND BAR.
Officer Commanding C Company.

CAPT. E. N. GARDNER, M.C.
Officer Commanding B Company.

talion Headquarters being in a small shelter against an orchard on the west of the road running through the centre of the Battalion front.

The barrage was rather erratic and seemed to fall on or near the forming-up line in the left and centre.

Junction Post was occupied by C Company and no trouble was encountered by D Company on the right, but fighting went on at close quarters in the enclosed ground west of Junction Post, while on the left A Company had established itself on the line ordered.

The position west of Junction Post was obscure all the morning. As far as could be gathered this ground had been occupied, but had been recaptured by a counter-attack.

On the following morning two platoons of B Company were put under command of Capt. Lavender of C Company to clear up the position on his left and secure the enclosed ground. This attack was ordered for 6.30 a.m., the troops only just reaching their places in time, owing to being shelled and gassed on the way up. The attack took place without artillery preparation and, the objectives being reached, Junction Post was thus secured.

To Capt. Lavender great credit is due for his handling of his company on the first morning and for his attack on the following day. For these operations he was awarded a bar to the Military Cross. It was, however, a great loss to the Battalion when, a few minutes after the completion of the attack, he got a machine-gun bullet in the right arm, and it was subsequently found to have lodged in his ribs.

In the two days' fighting the Battalion took 17 prisoners, 1 trench mortar and 6 machine-guns.

The losses were : killed, Capt. Eric Harvey, M.C., and Lieut. Jackson, other ranks 15 ; wounded, Lieut. Crucifix, other ranks 53 ; missing, other ranks 2.

Capt. Eric Harvey's death was a loss the Battalion could ill afford. The best of company commanders and the cheeriest of comrades, he displayed the utmost gallantry on every occasion. His disregard of danger inspired his men, who would go anywhere under his command. He was killed by a machine-gun bullet while walking back to his Company Headquarters from the front line in daylight. When the war broke out he was at Oxford, intending to take Holy Orders : his intentions were fulfilled in another sphere of service.

Lieut. Jackson, of D Company, had only been a short time with the Battalion, but this was long enough to show that he was a stout-hearted and capable officer.

The losses also included a Machine-Gun Battalion officer, Lieut. Clancy, who was killed on the left early on the first day.

Brig.-Gen. Pagan describes this action as a complete success, despite the heavy casualties.

"The Glosters fought," he says, "with stubborn determination, and their success under great difficulties . . . and where so many others had failed, was a very fine effort."

An hour or two after the completion of these operations the Germans put over a covey of 77's at short range on Battalion Headquarters, which was at once vacated for the open country, but not before one had hit a Battalion signaller and a second knocked some teeth out for the Commanding Officer and a third caught L/Cpl. Murray in the hand.

On relief on the same day a return was made to quarters outside Estaires for one night. The move forward over Aubers Ridge by the Oxfords necessitating a move forward to the posts known as Laventien.

Early in the morning Capt. Harvey was buried in the Estaires cemetery with full military honours. "Last Post" was blown and volleys were fired. The service was attended by most of the officers and the whole of A Company who, owing to the early hour, came on parade just as they had left the line, unshaven and with the mud of the trenches still on them. The service was none the less impressive on that account.

It was a curious coincidence that the men who were

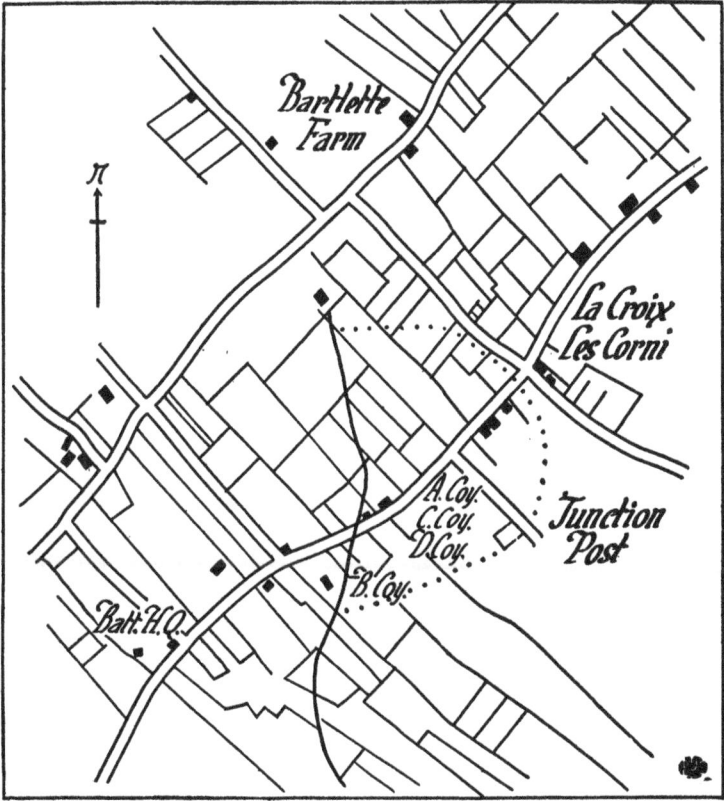

Attack on
Junction Post.

killed on September 30th, 1918, were buried in the cemetery north of Laventie, beside their comrades who fell on July 19th, 1916.

The Higher Command's prognostication as to Junction Post being the correct place to attack was entirely correct and thirty-six hours later the Brigade was moving forward again.

On the evening of October 3rd the Brigade was withdrawn to La Gorgue and there entrained in open trucks on the light railway for La Lacque, which was reached at 6 a.m.

On Lt.-Col. Christie Miller, M.C., proceeding to England, the command of the Battalion was taken over by Major R. H. Huntington, D.S.O. Lt.-Col. Christie Miller had been Commanding Officer since the death of Col. Lawson on June 24th. It was no easy task to succeed such a distinguished officer, but a combination of conscientiousness and courage quickly won for him the confidence and respect of all ranks, and the fact that the Battalion maintained its standard of efficiency through the trying months during which he controlled it, testifies to the value of his leadership.

CHAPTER XII

OCTOBER 5TH TO NOVEMBER 11TH, 1918

ON the night of October 5th/6th the Battalion went to Beauval. Here a re-union took place between Major Allen, one of the Battalion's dearest and oldest friends, and some of the officers of the 2/5th, including Capt. John Hunter and Capt. Sinclair.

From Doullens the troops then moved by train to the area west of Cambrai, camping in Bourlon Wood with Battalion Headquarters at the brick-kiln. The country was scoured and ravaged by the heavy fighting of 1917 and 1918. An opportunity was given of inspecting the wonderful concrete defences of the Hindenburg line and of exploring Bourlon Wood. It was here that the congratulatory message from the General Officer Commanding for the attack on September 30th, was read.

On the 14th a move was made to Proville, a village lying just south-west of Cambrai. The men were settled comfortably in a barn and the officers retired to a house in the same farm. As a convivial meal was being indulged in, a great tumult of coughing and sneezing was heard coming from the yard ; it transpired that the Germans had thoughtfully treated the stream to a dose of lachrymatory gas before leaving. A mysterious wire shortly after caught someone's attention, and on tracing this wire to its source, it was found to be connected up to an infernal machine which would have sent a large part of the Battalion sky high that night, had the discovery not been made.

The five days at Proville were spent in cleaning up the

139

battlefield ; it was an unpleasant task consisting mostly in burying dead men and horses. One sight will never be forgotten : it was the weird sight of half a dozen dead Britishers, inextricably mixed up with a similar number of dead Germans ; they had all killed one another in severe hand to hand fighting—some had their hands gripping each other's throats, others were transfixed with bayonets, others were blown to pieces by bombs. It was a haunting spectacle.

After a few days at Cagnoncles the Division went into action again, the 184th Brigade being in support.

At 6 a.m. on the 24th the Glosters moved forward and bivouaced in a sunken road. At 2 p.m. verbal orders were received from 184th Brigade Headquarters to attack the village of Vendegies and the high ground north-east of the Ecaillon river. The acting Commanding Officer issued his orders to companies in a quarry. Here was open warfare with a vengeance ; little or no time for detailed preparations ; verbal orders and counter orders ; and a general sense of haste and uncertainty.

The Battalion arrived after two hours very heavy marching at Bermerain, south-east of Vendegies at 5 p.m. No time was lost ; maps were scarce ; no one had the vaguest idea of the topography of the country, the position of the enemy, the situation of the other troops ; and, as though to add an extra difficulty, it was already sunset. The Battalion got into diamond formation facing east and moved forward. Scarcely had the move started than the enemy sent up red rockets and a tremendous bombardment opened.

To continue in Capt. Sinclair's own words :—

" My recollections at this point are somewhat vague as I was stunned by a 5.9 and getting to my feet again I was a trifle unsteady. I have dim recollections of pushing on to a sunken road with the Battalion in some sort of order. Then we all lost touch and were more or less lost. Anyhow, we seem to have done what was required of us, and the enemy cleared out of Vendegies and at dawn on the

CAPT. J. D. JOHNSTON, M.C.
Officer Commanding B Company.

CAPT. R. S. B. SINCLAIR,
M.C. AND BAR.
Officer Commanding A Company.

25th, after a night of confusion, darkness and considerable shelling, we reorganised on the high ground east of the village. We captured 16 prisoners and lost 2 killed, 25 wounded, the major part of our casualties having been suffered when starting from Bermerain. About 7 a.m. the 2/4th Royal Berks passed through and became the front line."

The 26th was consolidating the position and the Glosters remained in support until November 1st. Shell fire continued to be fairly heavy, but the Battalion suffered no further casualties. The next fifteen hours were memorable chiefly because they were the last hours during which the Battalion was under fire. At 5.15 a.m. the 61st Division attacked along the line of the Rhonelle river about one and a half miles in front of the Glosters' position. The attack was successful, the river was crossed and Maresches was practically taken. At 9 a.m. D Company moved forward to some high ground to observe enemy movements and apprise the Battalion of a possible counter-attack.

Midday the other three companies moved forward, taking up a position in a sunken road just east of the Rhonelle and a mile north of Maresches. Masks had to be worn during this advance as the enemy was throwing over a good ration of gas shells. At 5 p.m. the Battalion was ordered to attack eastward through Maresches and to occupy the high ground east of the village. Here again are Capt. Sinclair's words :—

" My own objective was some cross-roads east of Maresches, marked by a tall factory chimney and other buildings, and named St. Hubert. Meanwhile the men had a somewhat haphazard meal in the sunken road and D Company rejoined us. The objective was to be marked out for us by our artillery firing star shells, and we were to have a protective creeping barrage. At 7.30 p.m. we moved forward into a void of darkness—our only means of keeping direction was by compass, except for the bursting of the star shells. We were unable to keep up with the barrage ; moreover we lost touch with one another. We moved through the advanced line of our Divisional troops, over a field of turnips, in what was supposed to be diamond formation. I remember plunging through a hedge with the men and landing in an orchard, where we came under enemy fire. We rallied the men, fixed bayonets and charged into the darkness. We were certainly very far short of our official objective. Forms of Germans loomed up at us ; some of us got in front of our own Lewis guns ; some succeeded in bayonetting a few Germans. I deflected a German thrust with an ash stick—my revolver was clogged with mud—and things seemed to be in a pretty state of chaos. We took about 18 prisoners, who were sent to the rear. What exploits B and C Companies performed I do not know to this day. Things quietened down after this scrap and we dug ourselves in, having not the foggiest notion where we were or who was on our flanks or where the enemy was or what had happened to the rest of the Battalion. We were very much ' in the air.' However, after an anxious night, during which nothing happened, we were relieved by the Oxfords and then slept in an orchard waiting for the attack on an eleven mile front which was to take place at dawn."

This attack on the morning of November 2nd was made under cover of a barrage, with two companies forward and two in support. Everything went like clockwork and the operation was a complete success. 3 officers and 240 other ranks were captured, as well as 1 field gun, 1 minenwerfer and 21 machine-guns. The hold on Maresches was permanently established though it was heavily shelled by the retiring enemy. Capt. Sinclair was wounded during this operation and the Battalion's total casualties were 14 killed, 42 wounded, 14 gassed.

The Battalion was relieved in the line by the 13th Middlesex Regiment, 24th Division and marched to billets in Bermerain ; on the 3rd it moved to Avesnes-Les Aubert and formed for the time being part of Corps Reserve. On the 4th it was learnt that the enemy was still retiring and the day was spent in overlooking kit and equipment.

On the 5th the Battalion moved from Avesnes and arrived back at Bermerain where, on the following day, it received a congratulatory message from the Divisional Commander on its fighting spirit and general smartness.

Orders to move to Maresches were received on 7th, and then cancelled, but the move took place the following day. For the next three days steady training by companies was carried out, billets were cleaned and general salvage work done, and then came the historic 11th of November, and here it is best to quote the words of the Battalion Signalling Sergeant who actually was the first to receive the message from the operator.

" About 9 a.m. I went to the signal office for the usual test from Brigade and to synchronise my watch with Brigade Time. At 9.5 Brigade rang up on the DIII VE VE VE SB. The last two letters have an electric effect on an operator as they signify a ' priority message '—an order to move to another unhealthy spot, I thought. The operator gave the G and then the historic message came through :—

' Hostilities will cease at 11.00 hrs. to-day, Nov. 11th AAA. Troops will stand fast on line reached at that hour which will be reported to Corps HQ AAA Defensive precautions will be maintained AAA. There will be no intercourse of any description with the enemy AAA.' Never has a Morse code conveyed such satisfaction, such utter relief and joy. We in the office became almost delirious. An orderly was despatched at once to the Officers' Mess with the welcome tidings ; runners conveyed the news to Company Commanders who were drilling their men in the adjoining fields ; cheer after cheer came rippling faintly across to the office as the news was read out to the men."

Sgt. Child had the pleasure of an impromptu dance

with R.S.M. Spragg that would have shamed the *première danseuse* of a Parisian cabaret. The Sergeants' Mess was a lively place that night ; there was no bread, rum or fresh meat, but there were potatoes, carrots, parsnips, cabbages and sugar beet, and tea, the only beverage available, had a peculiarly intoxicating effect that night of nights.

No one has recorded how the officers behaved—perhaps no one remembers.

CHAPTER XIII

LOOKING BACK

RECOLLECTION, philosophers say, is the elixir of old age. Thus some of us, upon whom the blight of years is settling, look back at the days when we adventured and find there satisfaction for ourselves, a mutual link with erstwhile companions, a tilting ground it may be, but one where we fence with foils. Someone leans across the table ; " Do you remember," he asks, and whole vistas straightway open out and memories come crowding back so that even the eightpenny glass of tawny becomes a thing of peculiar mellowness. Do we remember ? Why, of course we do. There were the false heroics at the outbreak of war—urchins marching down Whitehall flag-wagging and beating tin cans—cheap songs about tramping feet and sweethearts bidding farewell—then came the posters of Belgian refugees and Kitchener pointing a menacing finger at you and me. That is how most of us were caught up in the current of things and without being able to give a definite explanation found ourselves one day soldiers. How we hated being told that we were doing our bit ! Then came the first appearance on parade : we had been soldiers for just one day and there was nothing soldierly about any of us except the oath we had taken. We fell in—there is no other word for it—wearing trilby hats, tweed caps, soft collars, golf coats, overalls, flannel trousers, dungarees, spats, black boots and canvas shoes. Just a few had a touch of military colour, thanks to Mr. Fox's patent puttees. Our civil occupations too were as various, ranging from commissionaires to K.C.'s, with a liberal seasoning of actors, schoolmasters and footpads. The first thing we learnt was the " about turn," that amazing gyration that recalls the impression of being thrown out of the lounge bar at the end of a convivial evening. Next came the " quick march," with body erect and carried evenly over the thighs and so on through all the gamut of those hardships to which the recruit is unwilling heir. We returned to our homes after that first day's training in a weary bewildered frame of mind, feeling more like prisoners on remand than free citizens, or possibly embryo brigadiers, and in our dreams we dreamed a dream about a gravelled square and a sergeant-major who possessed an original and explosive vocabulary, and we awoke to find ourselves marking time against the foot of the bedstead. Laboriously we learnt our squad drill and then followed our initial attempts at drilling other men.

Soldiering was so unnatural an element to some of us that we shunned its publicity ; we belonged to another vintage. Let us alone, we thought but dare not utter, in the middle of the rear rank, and we would have done anything the sergeant-major asked of us : we would have cleaned oily rifles in a dirty armoury : we would have hawked fruit in the Tottenham Court Road, or opened small " pollies " on a seaside pier : we would even have sewn buttons, if such things are sewn, on ladies' camisoles, for the duration of the war if only we were not asked to face a squad and drill it.

Later on when we became commissioned officers in an infantry regiment we simply had to overcome this aversion. Why did we not from the beginning aim to become Divisional Salvage Officers and so be able to put D.S.O. after our names without having to go through a course of shouting " at the halt on the left form close column of companies " and other such orders ? We remember how we were told that the first duties of a young officer were to be smart and to have a good word of command. The good word of command is all very well, but how to look smart with a pair of spiral puttees that would not conform to a pair of non-compliant calves was a problem that some of us never solved. Then, again, we remember the eternal confusion between left and right and how we longed to be allowed to give our orders from the rear so that our right and the platoon's right would not be at cross purposes and how grateful we were when the platoon, divining our intentions, disobeyed our orders and so saved us from piloting it into the officers' latrines or some other place not provided for in the drill book.

Two more ports, please—large ones.

That reminds one of the Orderly Officer. The Orderly Officer is to the Captain of the week what the bailiff is to the squire. He performs most of the duties for which the Captain of the week is responsible : he is, in fact, the latter's devil.

" If you have got a job to do, get someone else to do it," is one of the axioms of the Army, and it was never better exemplified than in the relationship of the two officials in question.

The Orderly Officer has to be a man of many parts : he has to attend sick parades and staff parades ; he sees guards and picquets mounted ; he visits regimental institutes, billets and cookhouses ; he is present during the issue of rations, and it is he who certifies the punctuality and adequacy of meals. For these purposes, he has to be a kind of amalgamation of commercial traveller, butcher, sanitary expert and philosopher. He must be able to differentiate fly-blows from soapsuds ; he must gauge the amount of sugar needed to sweeten the soldier's palate against a pound of tea ; he must know how many potatoes go to a dixie of stew ; he must judge the amount of creosote allowed to a latrine bucket ; he must ken the science of sousing camping kettles. To these accomplishments he must add the tact of an archbishop, the sympathy of a Harley Street specialist and the judgment of a Lord Chancellor.

One of the least appreciated and most ungrateful tasks of the Orderly Officer consisted in those days long ago of visiting huts while the men were breakfasting. Who does not remember that agitated halt outside each hut as the Corporal threw open the door and asked " Any complaints ? " Of course there were always complaints, but only very occasionally were they justified. On such occasions the Orderly Officer was sometimes called upon to intervene and to propitiate the disgruntled troops. Perhaps the fish, like the proverbial worm, had turned, and there lingered about the hut an aroma that was redolent of a foot inspection on a thundery afternoon : a new issue of rations had somehow or other to be procured and after a deferred meal the wretched Orderly Officer had to make a deposition to the Quartermaster on the habits of tinned fish and the next of kin.

Then there are the personal recollections—the men whom we meet again and with whom we talk over old times, and those whom we once knew who passed over in the great adventure. It is a curious fact that we incline, when thinking of the former, to revert to our training days ; when we speak of the latter, our thoughts nearly always carry us back to the fields of Flanders—we seem to hear the tramp of their feet upon the cobbled streets : we see a phantom of ruined cottages, stunted tree trunks, a countryside torn and twisted in its agonies, and some tiny rough-hewn crosses on the hillside where the poppies bend as the wind westers home.

Poignant memories are these. How we huddled together, our backs pressed against the fire bay in those dank trenches when the " minnies " began to drop and the earth trembled —the lull—the ominous " Stretcher bearers at the double " —the twilight fading into darkness—the " stand to " and then the sentries left looking across into the pitch black void—a patrol scrambling over the parapet and disappearing —the spasmodic, ceaseless rat-tat-tat—the waiting, always waiting, for the dawn.

Sleep—unbroken, dreamless sleep was a luxury unknown. Perhaps we dozed for half an hour on a narrow layer of mis-shapen sandbags in a semi-conscious delirium—dreamed that we were in No Man's Land, enmeshed in barbed wire—a thousand blue-grey figures with wreaths of yellow gas exuding from their nostrils, leered and leapt at us from a distant crater—our respirators were derelict—our bombs fizzled but would not leave our hands—our " cut-offs " were jammed. At last, we awoke to find ourselves lying face downwards on a sodden sandbag, taking cover behind a bundle of uncensored letters and going through the motions of the " rapid load " with a box periscope.

Let us get back in billets, we thought, where we can at least sleep, even if we have to lie on mattresses of brick and rubble—even if the sky is our roof and rats our only mess-mates. All we yearned for was to get away somewhere, anywhere, where we could just sleep and forget about shells, raids, wiring parties and gas alarms—where we could dream, perchance, of murmuring poplars, of gorse and laburnum bloom, of tender hands and kisses.

There was something about those few days in billets, after a tour of trench duty, intensely human—something that seemed to lift us above mere sordid materialism. The chances that we had all taken together had reduced us, so to speak, to a common denominator : we had become something essential to one another. When conditions were at their worst, we were wont to be cheerful : when we had to exist in mud and filth, one's thoughts were often in the clouds. We lived, as it were, in a complacent latitude that lies halfway between Heaven and Charing Cross.

The four or five days of pleasant indolence were soon spent and the bugle summoned us to parade again for another weary tour of trench routine.

We glanced along the ranks and missed a few faces that were there last time we went up the line. Who next ? we wondered.

Ah, well ! Whoever he may be, it is more than a little

to know that he brought the gift of happiness to others and that he belonged to a brotherhood where sorrow and gaiety were shared, and where, though absent awhile, he will abide with us for all time.

The sound of distant gun fire breaks the spell and evening spends her crimson light.   Fall in, for there are others who require sleep.

"THE CHEERYOHS."

CHAPTER XIV

DEPARTMENTAL NOTES

" THE CHEERYOHS "

IN the foundation of the " Cheeryohs " at that spot of blessed memory, Buire au Bois, Lieut. Frank Wooster was the chief conspirator. He actively concerned himself in providing the Battalion amusement by collecting all the available talent he could find, commandeering a pianoforte, " wangling " time off duty for rehearsing the artistes, and his efforts resulted in the formation of a very presentable troupe, with costumes and stage effects complete.

The setting of the first stage in the orchard at Buire au Bois lingers in the memory : the weather was beautifully fine and the peaceful surroundings were in sharp contrast with the scenes upon the Somme battlefield that the Battalion had just left. A great deal of credit is due to those who staged this debut, and the applause occasioned by the famous duettists, J. Hayes and J. Dredge, the melodious warblings of C. Blackburn and J. Morrison's " Admiral's Broom," made these items part of the troupe's stock repertoire for quite a long time. But there were others too : there was W. Sparrow in the humorous rôle, Dobbs, Vowles and Mace in their various capacities, and by no means last, L. Parker, the prolific piano puncher, who could apparently play anything from Crown and Anchor to a classical sonata. Behind the scenes was the producer, J. R. Little, who invented rhymes and other crimes as easily and as quickly as a rabbit begets its young.

The " Cheeryohs," whose name was only arrived at after much cogitation, kept together and resurrected themselves whenever prior engagements with their Teuton neighbours did not interfere. Cuts were made here, additions there, and the programmes improved both in quality and quantity. They were fortunate in retaining the services of the original members of the troupe for some considerable time, though apart from visiting other battalions at Buire au Bois, they had no further opportunities of performing again until the Battalion rested at Oost Houck before moving to the Ypres sector. When again the Battalion was. in rest on the Arras Front, successful appearances again took place. It was at this time that R.S.M. Spragg became virtually the father of the troupe, and well he nursed his child. Some good sketches and novel items were introduced that were very much to the tastes of the audience.

After this came a long interval of inactivity, culminating in those dark spring days of 1918, when there were more pressing engagements to attend to. Thus for a time the " Cheeryohs " became only a memory, sans props, sans costumes, sans everything.

The memory, however, lingered, and after hostilities had ceased and the Battalion was at Domqueur, at the end of November, the old idea was resuscitated. Thus the remnants of the original party, helped by the unstinted co-operation of the officers of the Battalion, blossomed forth as the " Yellow Dandies." There was plenty of time for rehearsal, and plenty of space for performances, so all stage effects were of a very much higher order than before, and some excellent entertainment was provided. The party consisted of Lieut. Chalk, the producer, Capt. Horton, Lieut. Horton, the American doctor who was then attached, Lieut. Pitcher, Lieut. Young (whose electrical and mechanical knowledge as well as his knowledge of make-up were invaluable), R.S.M. Spragg, the Drum Sergt. and Pte. Robson, the George Robey of the Battalion. Cpl. Little transferred his activities from producer to that of scenic

artist, piano puncher and writer of lyrics. It will thus be
seen that the new troupe included very, very few of the
original " Cheeryohs," such is the price of war.

It would be ungracious to omit mention of Sgt. Child.
He was " advertisement manager," and well he managed,
for Domqueur was plastered from head to foot with samples
of his well-known artistry.

It is impossible to remember everybody and everything
connected with these entertainments since they were
unofficial operations which do not figure in the War Diary.
If disappointment is caused because of some unintentional
omission surely there is a compensation in the fact of having
helped in so valuable a way to recreate the spirits of the
troops when worn and tired.

The entertainments which the " Yellow Dandies " gave
were superior in every sense to those given by the
" Cheeryohs," but it must be remembered that they were
produced under very different circumstances and it is not
to be doubted that the latter served their purpose just as well.
The " Cheeryohs," moreover, were unique in this respect,
that they were the only organised battalion party of the kind
in the Division at the time. Their final chorus, therefore,
makes a fitting curtain to this brief review :—

" Now we've come to the end of our music and gags,
We'll sing you the tune of the jolly old Brags.
It's one of the best every Gloster admits,
And full of melodious twiddley bits.
May we hear it again in the good times to come,
With happier hearts beating time to the drum,
When the peace that has been " upon indent " arrives,
And we all go on leave for the rest of our lives."

The Canteen

The regimental canteen exists for the use and abuse
of troops. Its importance on active service varies in
inverse proportion with the space allotted to it.

The Gloster Canteen did its work well : it always managed

to be where the Battalion or the bulk of the Battalion was ; it was always possible at the end of a perfect day to obtain a pair of laces or a writing pad.

It had a difficult rôle to fill, because it had to be mobile and yet it had to be capable of enormous expansion at times, and it sometimes happened that when its stock was at expansion limit, the stock of transport was just the reverse ; it was then that the troops resorted to abuse when, after a trek, they made a raid upon the Canteen only to find that there was a shortage of " gaspers." As a work of supererogation the Canteen Corporal always endeavoured to be as full of supplies as possible on pay days. When he failed, it was only his pachydermic qualities that enabled him to withstand the criticisms of the troops.

The Gloster Canteen had no particular history—it never made any. It was one of those things that was born to blush unseen. Its foundation stone, so to speak, was a goodly wooden chest, which contained a limited supply of most of the stock ingredients of a soldier's life, such as Woodbines, bootlaces and tinned salmon. This box travelled many, many kilometres. One day the troops would ·be resting, another trekking, another fighting under desperate conditions. Casualties befell them, drafts arrived ; some came, others went—but the canteen box, like Tennyson's brook, went on for ever.

This wonderful chest, particularly if the Canteen Corporal was an accomplished scrounger, was like a conjuror's hat. At the end of a march, it could produce things in the way of spare kit that would have set the Regimental Quartermaster Sergeant thinking, but he was the one man who was not allowed to see. It has been said that without soldiers there would be no justification for war ; is it not equally true that without canteens there would be no justification for soldiers ? The 2/5th Glosters without its canteen would have been like Hamlet without the Prince of Denmark—it simply could not have been done—and there must be many who feel that the old wooden chest that followed the

THE TRANSPORT SECTION.

A HEADQUARTERS GROUP.

Battalion from Laventie to the Somme, then to Arras, Ypres and St. Quentin, that never grumbled and always gave of its best, should repose in the Cathedral Close surmounted by a bronze effigy of the Canteen Corporal.

Catering for troops was no easy matter, as supplies were often limited and the demand unlimited and it was just in those conditions when it was so difficult to obtain stores, that the troops had to rely the more upon the resources of the Canteen.

But on the whole the 2/5th Glosters were well served, and both officers and men have good reason to remember the Canteen Corporal and his old wooden chest with gratitude.

THE TRANSPORT SECTION

To the men in the ranks the transport section counted for little. They seldom troubled to realise that but for the transport they would have had no rations at the end of a day's march, no blankets for the night's lodgings, no field kitchen to provide that hot meal, no canteen for that "gasper," no water cart from which to fill that empty water bottle, no medical stores and for that matter, no machine-guns to support their attacks or cover their withdrawal. A unit without transport would be in worse plight even than a ship without fuel : the latter could at least float, the former would in a very short while simply cease.

To officers, of course, transport connotes all the above, but they are only intimately acquainted with the department known as Officers' Mounts, probably, almost certainly, the least important from the Battalion's point of view.

In the 2/5th there were many of the officers' horses that had reputations of their own. There was, for instance, that lazy old trooper Tom ; then there was Lady, a spritely mare ridden by Capt. Hollington and Capt. Davis ; then there was Major Allen's mount, christened later Mary Allen ; and Kinkie, who had a racecourse reputation which it justified by depositing Capt. Tubbs in a gorse bush, and by carrying Capt. Dudbridge involuntarily past Stonehenge at high velocity ; then there was Tiny, a huge, docile and good-natured beast that could only be mounted in full kit with the aid of a step ladder—he was Col. Collett's mount in France. There was Fireworks, too, a rough-shod, sturdy animal ridden by Capt. Badcock and, because of its name, avoided by less daring horsemen. There were many others that escape the memory after all these years.

But when the word Transport is used officially it means something much wider : it comprises 2 officers, 1 sergeant, 1 corporal, 3 L/corporals and 40 men, 11 officers' mounts, 7 light draft, 9 heavy draft, 9 pack ponies and mules, 9 limbers, 1 mess cart, 1 medical cart, 2 water carts and 4 cookers. Horses are a necessary, but only a small part, of the whole ; they are just cattle, conforming to the schoolboy's definition, " big animals with fur coats and four legs, one at each corner."

The transport officers whom the Battalion best remembers were Capt. Cyril Cole, Lieut. Bright and Lieut. Davis. Capt. Cole went through the War and then became a victim to the influenza scourge that raged over Europe after the armistice.

Inspections involved the Transport men in any amount of work. There were the horses to be specially groomed, the limbers and carts to be washed and the dixies to be shone ; but the 2/5th Gloster Transport won a number of prizes in competitions for the best " turn out." On one of the few occasions when it was unsuccessful, the General had found one loose hair on one of the draft horses, and so they lost the prize literally by a hair's-breadth.

While the Battalion was in Buire au Bois sports were held and all kinds of races were indulged in. The cream of the day was the officers' race on mules. Tom Merrell fixed up a stand, mounted it and made a book ; the odds he laid against the Colonel are not recorded—all that is known for certain is that the bookie won. In order to give the mules a good send off, the Brigade Band was brought into requisition, with the result that most of the mules grew restive and several were non-starters. Then it was suggested that the Transport men should have a similar race and that the officers should take over the duties of the Brigade Band. As three parts of the officers did not know at which end of their instruments to blow, the start was not a thrilling affair and when the big drummer made a noise like beating a truss of hay, the mules became positively complacent and not at all inclined to race.

But the life of a Transport man does not consist only in grooming horses, polishing limbers and trundling along in rear of the Battalion. There was such a thing as bringing rations and ammunition up to the Battalion when it was in the Forward Zone, and as all important cross-roads and tracks in rear were well taped by the German guns, this duty was not exactly a picnic. On the whole the section was fortunate in the matter of casualties but the strain of these journeys lay not only in the casualties actually suffered, but in the knowledge that they might be suffered at any minute.

On one occasion, after taking rations to the Battalion, Lieut. Davis had instructions to call at Brigade Headquarters on the return journey. He succeeded, either by design or accident, in falling down a well, and had to be rescued by means of a rope. As his rescuers above heaved at the rope, they were encouraged to hear his voice getting louder and louder—" It's jolly good of you fellows," a lull and then, " they ought to put a cover on this —— hole." At length he was retrieved and was, with his transport men, regaled with some refreshment at Brigade Headquarters. If there was any grumbling after that incident, he always used to say, " Remember if I had not fallen down that —— place, you wouldn't have got that drink, so that's that."

Transport men on the whole, perhaps, did more scrounging than others, because they were more often in circumstances where there were opportunities for scrounging.

Many will remember " Sausage," as he was nicknamed, going into a shop in La Gorgue to get eggs. " Bon soir, madam," he said, " got any erfs ? " and he got them.

157

Too little has been written about the fortitude displayed by animals in the War. One instance is worth recording. Two mules were carrying a ration limber up the line when one of them was killed by a shell, the other stood perfectly still with his old ears wagging while he was released. He was then ridden back five or six miles to the transport lines to fetch another mule, hooked in again and taken up to complete the journey with the rations, and brought back to the Transport lines again, a journey of little less than sixteen miles. It was only when examined after the journey had been completed that it was found that he had been hit by shrapnel and had a deep wound of ten inches length in his hindquarters. It must have hurt him horribly every time he moved his hind leg. He was very stiff the following morning, but was able to walk to the railhead, whence he was sent to the veterinary hospital.

All honour to the Transport Section, to its officers and men and to those great dumb brutes who bore such sufferings and did not understand.

THE PADRE

In the Rev. Partum Milum few battalions had as good a Padre, no one had a better. He carried out his special duties with fervour and yet without ostentation, and he realised what many failed to understand, that to the man under fire a touch of human compassion is worth more than outward forms. Thus Padre Milum was to be found in the front-line trenches, in the support lines, at the aid post—anywhere, everywhere in fact where he could be of service to his fellow men. Associating, as he did, so intimately with all ranks, he could share in their humours, too, without ever cheapening his calling. As the Battalion was making its first train journey for the front, it was met by a train load of old hands going on leave. " Are we downhearted ? " they called. " No," came the chorus from the 2/5th led by the Padre. A laconic voice rejoined, " Then you —— soon will be."

LT.-COL. G. C. CHRISTIE MILLER, D.S.O., M.C.
Commanding Officer, June 1918—October 1918.

Services were held at various times when they were possible, and were always made to suit the convenience of the men. Once a Sunday service was held in an orchard which the farmer's wife had apparently reserved for her nag. She stormed and raved to such an extent that the nag began to storm and rave also, the scene resembling a circus rather than a parade service. However, the Padre quietened her with his best French : " Seelonce, seelonce, Madame." Often on a Sunday Padre Milum had a busy and exciting day. One Sabbath started with Communion celebrated in a ruin ; then there was an evening service out of the line at which 500 men attended, and which was interrupted by falling fragments from aircraft guns ; then came a service in the firing line, held under the parapet, then another in a post and lastly evening prayers with another detachment.

One Sunday the Padre arrived at the place where the Battalion was resting to find that sides were being picked for a football match. One side immediately picked him, the Sergeant-Major announcing that at the close of the game the Padre would conduct Divine Service. When the game was over the Padre shouted to the players and spectators, " Now, you beggars, this is the first game of football I've ever played on a Sunday, so it's up to you to stay to the service." They all stayed.

But Padre Milum was much more to the Battalion than the man who conducted services. He tells the story of how when accompanying Col. Balfour round the front line, the Germans started to send over aerial torpedoes. The Padre was determined not to move until the suggestion came from the Colonel. Presently Col. Balfour said hurriedly, " Come on, Padre, there'll be a devil of a trouble if you get killed." On getting safely back to Headquarters, the Colonel re- counted the incident to the Adjutant in these words, " They started a strafe and the Padre ran and I've only just caught him up."

Padre Milum in his wanderings between front line

trenches, rest camps and hospitals, saw an intimate side of life that the soldier seldom met with. On one occasion an old French woman asked him to go into her house to see what the Germans had left her. With tears in her eyes, she pointed to her best bonnet and her husband's silk hat, both bashed in. Through a window she espied a few German prisoners being led down the street. " Les canailles ! " she screamed at them.

On a beam in a dugout which he visited were the names of the German signallers who had previously occupied it before being driven out. The names ran thus : " Hans Fritz, Dec. 1914 ; Karl Jung, June 1915 ; Oskar Klatz, Dec. 1916." One of the victors had added below : " Na Pooh, fini. Buzzy off. April 1917."

He tells how, while the Battalion was at Laventie, three storks sat on the ruined church tower from evening till morning and how people regarded this as an omen that the war would last three months. There is surely just a touch of mysticism here.

One day he was showing photos of his wife and children to the Madame whose billet he was occupying. " Is Madame twenty-one years ? " she asks as she inspected the vignette of his wife. " Oui," said the Padre, unthinkingly and in his best French. " And how old are the children ? " she continued ; " M'sieur le Chapelaine married very young."

In his friendship with Father Buggins, the Roman Catholic Padre, Padre Milum showed a tolerant good fellowship that evaporated all sectarian differences. He was a true disciple of the Shavian doctrine that there is only one religion in the world, though there are many versions of it. " You daren't come to a Catholic service, Milum," said the former. " Yes, I dare, Buggins," replied Milum, " without even making the condition that you come to a Protestant one." So he accompanied the Roman Catholic Padre to " Benediction," and enjoyed it. A lighter side to their friendship was brought about when, owing to enemy shelling, they were compelled to sleep together in a cellar. Padre Milum's only comment on this side of war is, " Buggins' snoring is worse than guns."

Many were his experiences while on duty at Aid Posts : men, who were slightly wounded and glad to be alive ; others, shell-shocked with their minds wandering ; others, knowing that they were dying, giving him messages to send to their homes, and asking him to pray with them ; others again so far gone as to be beyond the power of recognition.

Padre Milum fulfilled his mission worthily, for he brought a touch of friendliness and good cheer to both officers and men wherever he went—entered into their humours, softened their distress and in his unobtrusive way, kept the Creator of all things alive in a world that was striving to destroy creation.

CHAPTER XV

MEMOIR OF A PRISONER OF WAR

MEMORY has been described by someone as the treacherous ally of invention. Bearing this statement in mind and conscious that after a lapse of many years the line dividing fact from fable grows dim in outline, Capt. Barnes has written the following reminiscences of his life as a prisoner of war.

" I was captured on the second day of the ' Big Push,' March 1918, under the railway embankment that runs behind Holnon Wood. While a sergeant was disarming and placing me under escort, a German infantryman, advancing along the railroad, fired point blank at me and missed from a distance that could not have been more than fifteen yards. Till then I had always regarded myself as the world's worst marksman ; from then onwards I placed myself second. This was the last rifle shot that I heard during the war, though later I heard others under different circumstances.

" My captors were not bad fellows. I dare say they were even grateful to me for affording them an official reason for deserting the firing line for a time. They allowed me to lie down for some time before taking me back and on the journey I was given frequent rests, since, owing to a freely-bleeding wound, I was not in very first-class condition for walking any distance.

" As my escort and I plodded slowly back, we naturally went over a good deal of familiar ground and the road leading up to and through Holnon village was a shambles indeed. The surface was torn and scarred by shell-holes, and bodies lay strewn in all directions and in every sort of attitude. Many of the upturned faces were recognisable ; nearly all wore the pallor of death, though in one or two instances an eyelid quivered as though the spirit was loath to leave its tenement. I was not allowed to tarry, except in the case of one man who, though quite helpless, was conscious : in this case I did prevail upon my escort to improvise with some reluctance a stretcher, and upon this the poor fellow was taken along with us.

" The Germans had established a forward dressing station in what had been our front line at Gricourt, and it was here that I was first taken. I was placed in a dugout, where I spent the night in company with a number of wounded Germans, whose guttural groans sounded rather like the bath water running away. This sound mingling with the thunder of artillery outside as it grew more and more distant was my requiem that night. Brilliant sunshine ushered in the next morning and I was allowed to come up into the open, where I lay on a grass bank. The tide of battle had by then swept many miles westwards, leaving very little evidence of the stupendous struggle behind it. There was a German Padre standing close by, with whom I attempted to open conversation, but apparently his ideas on Christian charity and brotherhood, all-embracing as they may have been, did not extend to the hated English, for he turned quickly away with a scowl and a stentorian grunt. Thus I was brought suddenly to realise my altered circumstances ; less than twenty-four hours ago I had been a dashing infantry officer—now I was but an ignominious captive : yesterday I was even worth shooting at—now I was not even worth speaking to. But if there were no Christians among German padres, there were sportsmen among German soldiers. A square-jowled Tommy, as he ambled past, smoking a cigarette, looked at me and understood my need. He immediately broke his cigarette in two and gave me one half.

"All that day I lay there, unfed and unattended by any medical man, the only food that I had had since my capture being some bully beef from a tin, which, by an act of Providence, I had stuffed into my pocket when the Battalion started to move back from Holnon Wood. Depressed in spirit, hungry and with a throbbing wound still undressed, I managed only with difficulty to crawl down into the dugout again, where I lay down and meditated on my past life. Just when I had decided against my chances of living, like the gunner of the little ' Revenge,' to fight again and strike another blow, a German orderly came down to tell me that a wagon was coming in the evening to take me back further. He was a first-rate fellow. He did his best to bind up my arm roughly with a piece of field dressing and he gave me some much needed food. Further than this, after the wagon had come and had conveyed me to a place about a mile and a half back, this good Samaritan later the same evening walked all the way there in order to find out how I was faring and to bring me some more fodder. My memory of my new lodgings is that I slept the night in a kind of yard, the ground floor of which resembled nothing so much as the bottom of a parrot cage, but without the sawdust.

"On the third day of my captivity I was moved again to a biggish town, Bellenglese, I think, where a number of wounded prisoners had been segregated. It was here that I received my first medical attention in the form of an operation and my arm was at last effectively bandaged. From this time onwards, for a matter of two months, persistent sleeplessness began to affect me.

"After a day and a night in this place we were all entrained for Germersheim, a small town in South Germany. The journey took two or three days and its discomforts are indescribable. There were at least thirty of us packed into a closed van of the normal horse-box size. We were all more or less seriously wounded and many of us were unable to stand. We had nothing to lie on except the bare floor of the van. The nights were chilly and we had not a blanket between us. We were shunted here and shunted there, and we had no chance of seeing where we were going or how fast we were travelling for there was not a window of any description in the van. There we lay in pitch darkness, shivering with cold and groaning at every jolt of the train. One man, who lay with both legs broken, died on the first day of the journey and so for several hours we had to travel with a corpse as a fellow-passenger. The only respite we had was when, at intervals, too rare for our liking, we were served out with cans of nondescript soup.

" At last we arrived at Germersheim. The walking cases were formed up in fours and marched through the town to a prisoner hospital. By this time I had degenerated into a stretcher case. I was operated on again directly I reached hospital, and after regaining consciousness found myself in a ward with some twenty other British officers. My arm was now tightly strapped up in a cradle, a large wire contraption that compelled me to keep my elbow and wrist bent at impossible angles. My worst experience of prison life began from now, and lasted until I was moved to Karlsruhe some months later.

" The Germans were short of staff and short of medical stores. Operations were, therefore, performed nearly always without any kind of anaesthetic, and the groans and yells that issued from the operating theatre are unimaginable. Wounds were bound up in paper bandages and were left unattended for days, even weeks, at a time ; the dirt was appalling ; the same bed sheets did service for two or three consecutive months. With only paper for bandages and with wounds suppurating like dripping taps, the condition of the bedclothes can be easily imagined. Things became, in the soldiers' patois, ' distinctly chatty.'

" I began at this time to develop a form of functional paralysis which later on resulted in my losing the use of all my limbs and my sight, but before it reached its worst stages I remember lying on my back unable to move my arms and watching the reconnoitring patrols of those light drab coloured insects that we soldiers knew so well, working along the seam of the grimy sheet that covered me. Our diet was spare and disproportionate. We had as much beer as the most confirmed toper could wish for, but it was beer only in colour and name ; in taste, it was like the swill from a rain-water butt and unlike my bed sheets there was no suggestion of ' hops ' in it. Solid food was less generously bestowed. Our staple course was soup into which a few errant potatoes had sometimes strayed. Occasionally, as a special relish, we were given fallen apples ; we regarded these in their double sense as windfalls.

" Those among the prisoners who could walk were allowed to exercise in the yard. Some genius among them gathered the fluffy insides of the thistles that abounded there, added water and kneaded the mixture into a pulp and then baked it on a stove. In this way we were able to supplement our scanty rations, an instance of how lack of civilisation causes a throwback to primitive habits. Once or twice a week, small pieces of sparsely-meated bones found their way into the usual ' consommé.' These bones bore no resemblance either in size or shape to any bones or joints that one associates with butcher's meat. This fact, coupled with the fact that no domestic animal of any sort was ever seen during our captivity, made us wonder. Verily ours was a ' cat and dog ' existence, if there ever was one.

" The Doctor at Germersheim may not have been a Prussian, though he was certainly a very good imitation as both in appearance and behaviour he displayed all the attributes that are associated with that vintage. The way in which he conducted his professional visits to our ward was amusingly callous. His method of procedure was to stand at the foot of No. 1 bed and yell the question ' Wie Gehts ? ' (which, being interpreted is a short way of asking ' Are you better ? '). No. 1 would answer in perfect German, ' Yah.' Whereupon the doctor would grunt ' Gut,' and pass on. At No. 2 bed he paused and yelled the same question, and No. 2 would reply ' Nein.' The doctor would rejoin ' Gut,' and pass on to the third bed, and so on round the entire ward.

" There was a corporal in charge of the ward. He was a taciturn looking fellow without any sense of humour or honesty (he stole most of my tobacco). It was one of his duties to warn us for the operating theatre. He would look at me and say, ' Bar-nes ' (pronouncing the name in two syllables), ' verbunden ' : and to illustrate his meaning he would move his hand round and round his arm as though unwinding a bandage. I would then be lifted out of bed and placed on a wheeled ambulance which we called the tumbril. Then I was wheeled out of the ward, and my fellow prisoners would softly whistle the andante section from Chopin's ' Marche Funebre ' as the cortège left the room. Directly I was in the passage outside I was greeted by the groans emitted from the operating theatre.

" The operating theatre itself had the appearance of a slaughter house : there was the doctor, wearing a large white leather apron, generously bespattered with blood, and holding a large rusty scalpel in his hand ; there was also a horrible looking Frau, standing some five feet ten inches in height and proportionately broad in the keel, who menacingly dangled a large pair of cutter's scissors. British Tommies could often be heard muttering as she passed along the corridors, ' There goes that —— old witch.' At least it sounded like that.

" I remember a Frenchman who lay in the bed next to mine. He was very badly wounded and very ill. That morning he had been given a rather violent aperient and it was while the corporal was washing up the dishes in the distant corner of the ward after our midday repast, that the Frenchman sent up an urgent S.O.S. He shouted excitedly to attract the corporal's attention, but the latter merely looked round in an abstracted way and then continued with his dish-washing. Some fifteen minutes later, when the plates were all dried and put away, he came across to the Frenchman's bedside and asked him what he wanted. 'Ah, eet ees too late, la la,' was the cryptic reply. The unfortunate Frenchman lay thus without any further attention for the rest of the day and so one more horror was added to our captivity.

"After many weeks of this kind of life, parcels from those at home (God bless them !) began to arrive and so our bitterest privations—fat, sugar and tobacco—were alleviated.

"What with our improved circumstances and our unfailing sense of humour, the dirt and even the operations we came to regard as minor inconveniences.

"With two or three others I was in the last batch to be moved to Karlsruhe. Karlsruhe had been a concentration camp for prisoners of war for some long time. The consequence was that by the time we arrived there, there was a very efficient organisation in working order. Some American prisoners had taken over the prisoner side of the camp ; they had formed a good library from the numerous books which had been sent over ; they made a pool of all the Red Cross parcels (private ones we kept for ourselves), and distributed their contents to all the prisoners ; they were also allowed to run concerts and other entertainments in the evenings with the single restriction that they were not allowed to sing or play ' God Save the King.'

"Under these circumstances life became so reasonable that I have ever since had a profound respect for the organising capacity of Americans. The hospital belonging to the camp in which I was placed was clean and well tended. The doctor in attendance there was a first-class fellow and a very considerable amateur musician. He and I had many a talk about Beethoven and Brahms. Moreover, the hospital orderly who tended me turned out to have been a waiter at the Café Royal for fifteen years prior to the War, so that we could talk about Piccadilly and Leicester Square in a way that made us close friends.

"Night after night, British bombing planes on their way to Mannheim used to pass over us and the Germans put up a tremendous barrage. This was the only thing that reminded us that a war was still going on.

"Not long before the Armistice, I contracted influenza which developed into pneumonia. I was therefore packed off to the town hospital where people were expected to die. But my good fortune did not desert me. The nurse who looked after me was a saint if ever there was one. She tended me night and day ; she gave up a large portion of her own scanty rations in order that I might get the best that was available ; she bought wine for me out of her own pay. 'He go *tod* to-night,' I heard her whisper with tears in her eyes to my nearest bedfellow. But this was the only case in which I disappointed her and I know she was glad. She named me her Doctor of Roses and I called her my Lady of the Snows—but that is another story.

"The Armistice was declared. The attendants rushed in to tell us and tore the Prussian buttons from their caps.

"That night some wild young cadets, sorry, I suppose, to miss the fun of the war, trained a machine-gun on the hospital windows, but our beds were moved out of the line of fire.

"There is little more to tell. Owing to difficulties of transport and as I was a stretcher case, it was not until well into December that I was repatriated.

"First I was taken to Freiburg. I was accompanied there by my hospital attendant, a huge fellow whom I called Hindenburg. He and I together consumed the entire intoxicants of the establishment at which we stayed, and though they consisted of only one solitary quart bottle of Chartreuse, I nevertheless felt very much the better for it. My Hindenburg there left me and I proceeded to Colmar, where I spent the night at the village inn. I arrived there in the midst of festivities which the Alsatians had organised in celebration of their redemption. Young men and maidens, all dressed up in their picturesque native costume, came to ask me if they might use the room in which I lay for a dance. I have never seen such a galaxy of pretty girls nor have I ever witnessed such care-free dancing as on that night, and I wondered for the minute whether I was just an ordinary soldier returning from captivity or a Trojan hero surrounded by syrens. Between each dance the girls left their partners to cluster round me and ply me with questions about my captivity. Their very spontaneity dispelled embarrassment, and war had never seemed so sweet. However, all good things come to an end and on the morrow I was again moved, this time under the auspices of the American Red Cross, and taken to Calais.

"The boat took me from Calais to Dover and while the steamer was ploughing its way across, I could not help contrasting the journey with the one I made when first the Battalion went to France. Then, everyone wore a life-belt, lights were hooded, destroyers steamed beside us and enemy submarines lurked about ; everyone spoke in a suppressed whisper : the future was obscure.

"Now we steamed back without a thought for to-morrow, with decks and cabins brightly illuminated, with loud talk and laughter, with the Straits secure and free again.

"At Dover we were entrained for Waterloo and then we were driven in ambulances to the Great Central Hotel, which had been converted into a military hospital.

"During my nine months' captivity some things struck me most forcibly. Firstly, I was surprised to find how few Germans could speak our language : I had always been given to understand that the German curriculum of education included a very liberal study of foreign languages and especially English. It may be so, but during the whole of my captivity I met only two or three who could speak English and this only in a very limited degree, and about the same number to whom I could make myself understood. Secondly, whereas I had always imagined that their discipline was iron in its rigidity, I found it exactly the reverse. A general slackness was noticeable ; the non-commissioned officers and orderlies with whom I came into contact dressed in a slovenly way and observed none of the decorum that we associate with the well-disciplined soldier. This outraged my own 'well-known punctiliousness' in *la mode militaire*. The respect shown to officers was at times negligible ; more than once I witnessed an altercation between the hospital orderly and the Medical Officer. On such occasions they would stand up against one another with their noses almost touching and shout at the tops of their voices, though, what sorts of compliments they were paying one another, my knowledge of their language did not enable me to more than surmise.

" Another salient feature was what appeared to be a general lack of interest in the War. In March when I was first captured, and when the German armies had the best of the argument, we were treated with scorn. When matters began to go the way of the Allies, the haughty and arrogant demeanour gave way to obsequiousness. But the vast majority did not speak about the War, did not read the papers, and appeared to take little interest in the course of events.

" The willingness, even the joy, with which the abdication of the Kaiser was accepted by the Southern Germans was also a significant fact. It seemed to be regarded rather as a happy release from an intolerable domination.

" On our side, the sense of humour which always came out in someone, even under the worst circumstances and our phlegmatic way of taking whatever came our way, made me realise what is meant by the strength of the unemotional Englishman. Comparing our demeanour under adversity with that of the Germans in similar circumstances and with that of others of the Allies, I became convinced that however long the War lasted we were bound to win in the end, and that the British were the backbone of the Allied cause.

" I have said that the Germans treated us with arrogance and indifference, especially while their armies were advancing. The handling of wounded prisoners was certainly rough and ready, and there were not many traces of human fellow-feeling. But though matters may have been different with unwounded prisoners, I must say in fairness that I never saw nor experienced any occasion of intentional ill-treatment. In fact, I found that the German " man in the street " very much resembled ourselves. He was bored to tears with fighting and was merely a cog in a machine that he could neither control nor understand. He loved his home and loved peace just as we do, and as I have previously recorded, both German men and women could prove by acts of kindness and sacrifice, that humanity and sportsmanship make stronger claims upon the actions of mankind, than national prejudices.

"If the War has taught us anything, surely it is this—that however much our material interests may differ, there is a common factor somewhere deep down in the hearts of all of us, and the spirits of those who crossed over in those dire days still counsel us to build up our sum of life upon it and so prosper God's kingdom on earth."

SERGT. E. C. GIBBS.
Hon. Treasurer, Battalion History
Committee.

SERGT. J. H. GURNEY.
Hon. Secretary, Battalion History
Committee.

THE ANNUAL RE-UNION

Les amis de mes amis sont mes amis. Such a spirit led
men to the battlefields ; such a spirit made it imperative
they they should re-unite after war had gathered in its
harvest and the reapers had gone their way.

So on September 16th, 1919, nearly 400 members of the
Battalion under the chairmanship of its erstwhile Commanding Officer, Lt.-Col. the Hon. A. B. Bathurst, met at
dinner in the Shire Hall, Gloucester, to renew old and
honoured friendships.

Under an organising Committee consisting of Lt.-Col.
G. F. Collett, D.S.O. (President), Sgt. E. C. Gibbs (Treasurer), C.Q.M.S. E. W. Jones (Secretary), together with
Capt. and Q.M. W. E. Tomlins, Lieut. and Q.M. J.
Canavan, C.S.M. W. C. Allaway, C.Q.M.S. R. J. Trigg
and Sgt. H. W. Webb, the gathering was established as an
annual event and the dinner now takes place alternatively
at Gloucester and Cheltenham on the second Saturday in
October.

One result of these meetings has been a unanimous desire
to have the story of the Battalion set out in book form—a
wish that was fulfilled at the Re-union Dinner, October 1930.

In the words of Cicero, *Amici rebus adversis probantur*
(adversity is the test of friendship) ; and for this reason,
if for no other, the volume will have an honoured place
among the shelves of those whom it most concerns.

" *Mehr licht,*" spoke Goethe as the hand of death gripped
him ; " More light," cry our preachers and our politicians,
in a world riven with discord—but the common cause is
lacking. The true purpose of this book and of these re-
unions is to recapture something of a spirit that grows
fugitive as the years recede and to re-kindle the memory of
those who have passed beyond, for they have seen the light.

LIST OF FATAL CASUALTIES

* Panel. † Column.
In those cases where the place of burial is not known, the Memorial has been given.

Name	Name of Cemetery or Memorial	Plot	Row	Grave	Date of Death
Acton, Pte. T. H., 18662 ...	Memorial in Pozieres British Cemetery		40*	2†	31-8-18
Adams, L/Cpl. E. F., 240193	Landrecies British Cemetery		A	63	4-11-18
Adams, Pte. S. R., 30196 ...	Rue du Bois Military Cem., Fleurbaix	2	D	2	30-9-18
Agg, Pte. R. J., 4651 ...	Pont du Hem Military Cemetery, La Gorgue	2	A	17	25-9-16
Alcock, A/L.Sgt. F., 267505	Rue du Bois Military Cem., Fleurbaix	2	E	7	30-9-18
Aldous, L/Cpl. C. B., 242060	Villers en Cauchies Communal Cemetery		B	15	2-11-18
Aldridge, Pte. C., 37884 ...	Memorial in Dud Corner Cemetery, Loos		61*	2†	19-4-18
Aldridge, L/Sgt. G., 202291	Memorial in Pozieres British Cemetery		40*	1†	31-8-18
Allanby, L/Cpl. C. E., 242166	St. Venant Robecq Road British Cemetery, Robecq	4	E	10	19-4-18
Andrews, Pte. J. C., 260235	Faubourg d'Amiens Cem., Arras	6	A	21	10-11-17
Angus, Pte. L. D., 5800 ...	Rue du Bacquerot No. 1 Military Cem., Laventie	1	L	16	27-7-16
Apperley, Pte. W. G., 241311	Gloucester Cemetery	War Graves N. G. 1211			19-1-19
Apthorp, Sgt. W. T., 267304	Roye New British Cemetery	3	F	3	6-6-18
Arkell, Pte. F. J., 240961 ...	Pozieres British Cemetery Memorial		40*	2†	21-8-18
Arnot, 2nd Lt. C.	Memorial in Tyne Cot Cem., Passchendaele		72*	1†	23-3-18
Ashley, L/Cpl. W., 242014	Pozieres British Cemetery Memorial		40*	1†	21-8-18
Askew, Cpl. A. H., 3777	Laventie Military Cemetery	2	F	12	31-8-16
Atkinson, Pte. W. S., 242430	Memorial at Arras		6*	16†	5-10-17
Averis, Pte. P. G., 241255...	Memorial in Tyne Cot Cem., Passchendaele		73*	1†	22-8-17
Badcock, Capt. M. F. (M.C.)	Memorial in Pozieres British Cemetery		40*	1†	27-8-18
Bailey, Pte. F., 260221 ...	Sunken Road Cemetery, Villers Plouich		A	8	9-12-17
Baker, Pte. A., 202505 ...	Memorial in Tyne Cot Cem., Passchendaele		73*	1†	14-9-17
Baker, L/Cpl. C. H., 240478	Memorial in Pozieres British Cemetery		40*	1†	31-8-18
Baker, Pte. J. J., 202976 ...	Querenaing Communal Cem.	1	A	6	2-11-18
Baker, Pte. W., 201305 ...	Vis-en-Artois British Cem., Haucourt	6	H	4	2-6-18
Baker, Sgt. W. H., 200162	Bermerain Communal Cem.		B	7	30-10-18
Ballinger, Pte. B., 202187	Memorial in Tyne Cot Cem., Passchendaele		73*	1†	27-8-17
Barber, Pte. T., 34585 ...	St. Venant Robecq Road British Cemetery, Robecq	3	C	7	23-6-18
Barnes, Pte. H., 5809 ...	Memorial in Dud Corner Cemetery, Loos		61*	8†	21-6-18
Barnett, L/Cpl. H. W., 267159 ...	St. Venant Robecq Road British Cemetery, Robecq	1	E	3	29-4-18

Name	Name of Cemetery or Memorial	Plot	Row	Grave	Date of Death
Barnfield, Pte. H. C., 241134 ...	Brown's Copse Cemetery, Roeux	4	B	10	5-11-17
Barrett, Pte. T., 260220	Memorial in Pozieres British Cemetery		40*	2†	21-3-18
Barrow, Pte. J. McM., 200355 ...	Merville Communal Cem. Extension	1	D	87	11-8-18
Bartholomew, Pte. P., 33640 ...	Memorial in Pozieres British Cemetery		40*	2†	21-3-18
Barton, Cpl. R. J., 242001 ...	Nesle Communal Cemetery		C	15	2-4-17
Baulch, Pte. F., 19417	Rocquigny Equancourt Rd. British Cem., Manancourt	7	A	4	9-12-17
Bawden, Pte. D. F., 267367 (M.M.)	Memorial in Dud Corner Cemetery, Loos		61*	3†	25-4-18
Baylis, Pte. W. F., 37495 ...	Vieille Chapelle New Military Cemetery	4	A	4	18-4-18
Bayliss, Pte. W. J. L., 24442 ...	Memorial in Pozieres British Cemetery		40*	2†	31-3-18
Beach, L/Cpl. G., 16428 ...	Brown's Copse Cemetery, Roeux	4	B	5	19-11-17
Beak, Pte. A., 4552	Cambridge Boro Cemetery	Site D		2889	8-10-16
Beaumont, Pte. C. T., 5140 ...	Memorial in Thiepval				26-11-16
Bell, Pte. J., 235216	Memorial in Tyne Cot Cem., Passchendaele		73*	1†	27-8-17
Bell, Pte. W., 241289 ...	St. Venant Robecq Road British Cemetery, Robecq	1	A	11	17-4-18
Bennett, Pte. A. R., 2793 ...	St. Vaast Post Military Cemetery, Richebourg	8	J	12	13-7-16
Bennett, Pte. S. C., 241229 ...	Aire Communal Cemetery	2	F	27	16-8-17
Berry, Cpl. W. G., 200157... ...	Rue Du Bois Military Cemetery, Fleurbaix	2	E	1	30-9-18
Bevins, Pte. H. W., 38238 ...	Memorial in Pozieres British Cemetery		40*	2†	31-3-18
Bird, Pte. F. J., 27357	Arnos Vale, Bristol	M.M.		201	5-5-18
Birt, Pte. G. L., 241077 ...	Chapelle British Cemetery	2	A	1	29-4-17
Bishop, Pte. R. B., 4837 ...	Memorial in Dud Corner Cemetery, Loos		61*	3†	4-9-16
Blackmore, Pte. T., 30032 ...	Villers Bretonneux Military Cemetery, Fouilloy	15	C	8	21-3-18
Blackwell, L/Cpl. R., 240447 ...	Vadencourt British Cem., Maissemy	1	C	88	7-4-17
Blake, Pte. F., 5153	St. Sever Cemetery Extension, Rouen	Blk. 0.2	P	5	27-11-16
Blake, Pte. H. J., 4680 ...	Contay British Cemetery	7	A	29	28-11-16
Blake, Pte. W., 4980	Memorial in Dud Corner Cemetery, Loos		61*	3†	15-8-16
Blanchard, Capt. F. J.	Aire Communal Cemetery	3	B	8	1-6-18
Bland, Cpl. A. E., 242156 ...	Brandhoek New Military Cemetery	1	E	14	4-9-17
Blane, Pte. H., 5855	Merville Communal Cem.	4	P	9	1-7-16
Blighton, Pte. F. G., 267311 ...	Villers Bretonneux Military Cemetery, Fouilloy	14	B	3	21-3-18
Bloomfield, Pte. H., 260144 ...	Memorial in Tyne Cot Cem., Passchendaele		73*	1†	16-8-17
Blyth, 2nd Lieut. A. F. ...	Memorial in Tyne Cot Cem., Passchendaele		154*	2†	22-8-17
Bond, Pte. J. H., 241029 ...	Vadencourt British Cem.	1	C	87	7-4-17
Boucher, Cpl. H. H., 202982 ...	Cross Roads Cemetery, Fontaine-au-Bois	1	H	17	1-11-18
Brain, L/Cpl. H. P. G., 2801 ...	Pont du Hem Military Cemetery, La Gorgue	2	A	18	25-9-16

Name	Name of Cemetery or Memorial	Plot	Row	Grave	Date of Death
Bridge, Pte. H. G., 266714	Laventie Military Cemetery	4	D	1	30-9-18
Brien, Pte. F., 241841	Duisans British Cemetery	5	D	8	26-11-17
Brimble, Pte. B. J., 202616 ...	St. Venant Robecq Road British Cemetery, Robecq	1	E	24	19-4-18
Brinkworth, Pte. W. E. C., 4635 ...	Regina Trench Cemetery, Courcelette	1	D	22	24-12-16
Britton, Pte. A. H., 201484 ...	Chapelle British Cemetery	2	A	5	30-4-17
Brookes, Sgt. F. J., 2802	Merville Communal Cem.	11	A	47	17-7-16
Brooks, Pte. E. W., 241588 ...	Memorial in Pozieres British Cemetery	40*		2†	21-3-18
Brooks, Sgt. M., 8006	Memorial in Dud Corner Cemetery, Loos	60*		2†	18-4-18
Brown, Pte. R., 39063	Memorial in Dud Corner Cemetery, Loos	61*		3†	24-4-18
Brown, Pte. W. H., 267518 ...	Memorial in Thiepval				24-4-18
Bryer, Pte. C., 241921 ...	Memorial in Berks Cem. Extension, Ploegsteert	5*		7†	11-8-18
Buckman, Pte. C. C., 203469 ...	St. Venant Robecq Road British Cemetery	4	C	13	30-5-18
Bugler, 2nd Lieut. L. H. ...	Shirehampton Cem., Glos.			895	25-3-18
Bullock, Pte. C. J., 9956	Memorial in Louverval Mil. Cemetery, Doignies	6*		1†	2-12-17
Burlton, Pte. E. L., 201935 ...	Memorial in Pozieres British Cemetery	40*		2†	31-3-18
Butcher, Pte. A. L., 203075 ...	Memorial in Pozieres British Cemetery	40*		2†	21-3-18
Calbreath, Pte. B., 266629 ...	Aire Communal Cemetery	2	F	6	23-4-18
Cambray, L/Cpl. W., 4589 ...	Memorial in Dud Corner Cemetery, Loos	61*		1†	21-6-16
Campbell, Pte. W. J., 38384 ...	St. Venant Robecq Road British Cemetery	4	E	12	29-4-18
Cardy, Pte. T. J., 2981	Rue du Bacquerot No. 1 Military Cem., Laventie	2	G	18	4-6-16
Careless, Pte. E., 242406 ...	Vermand Communal Cem., Buried among Civilians			2	5-4-17
Carney, Pte. D., 38231 (D.C.M.) ...	Memorial in Pozieres British Cemetery	40*		2†	21-3-18
Carr, Pte. F., 38212	Aire Communal Cemetery	2	J	16	10-5-18
Carter, Pte. F. T., 267005 ...	Memorial in Dud Corner Cemetery, Loos	61*		3†	24-4-18
Carter, Pte. R. J., 202369 ...	Bishops Stortford Cemetery	A	14	20	18-2-19
Caunt, Pte. A., 38209	Memorial in Dud Corner Cemetery, Loos	61*		3†	24-4-18
Chapman, Pte. A. L. G., 31420 ...	Sunken Road Cemetery, Fampoux	2	A	5	23-11-17
Chappin, Cpl. J., 242058 ...	Vadencourt British Cem.	1	C	47	7-4-17
Chorley, Cpl. F. J., 240851 ...	Grevillers British Cemetery	3	A	7	17-5-17
Clark, Cpl. C., 202584	Villers Bretonneux Military Cemetery	15	B	10	30-3-18
Clarke, Cpl. A. J., 30478 ...	Aval Wood Military Cem., Vieux Berquin	1	BB	8	11-8-18
Clarkson, Pte. A., 5938	Pont du Hem Military Cemetery, La Gorgue	2	A	15	25-9-16
Coe, Pte. W., 5869	Pont du Hem Military Cemetery, La Gorgue	2	B	15	16-10-16
Cole, Capt. C. L.	Etaples Military Cemetery	45	C	14	14-3-19
Cole, Lieut. C. S.	Royal Irish Rifles Grave-yard, Laventie	2	J	5	19-6-16
Cole, Pte. E., 37395	Memorial in Pozieres British Cemetery	40*		2†	21-3-18

Name	Name of Cemetery or Memorial	Plot	Row	Grave	Date of Death
Cook, Pte. A. D., 203481 ...	Memorial in Pozieres British Cemetery		40*	2†	21-3-18
Cooke, Pte. A. W., 8095 ...	Laventie Military Cemetery	2	A	9	80-6-16
Coombes, Sgt. A. L., 200150	Tyne Cot Cemetery, Passchendaele	5	D	18	27-8-17
Corben, Pte. H. G., 204095	Memorial in Berks Cem. Extension, Ploegsteert		5*	7†	22-8-18
Corbett, Pte. J. A., 39007	Ovillers Military Cemetery, Ovillers-la-Boisselle	17	A	10	25-8-18
Cordell, Sgt. G., 202262 ...	Memorial in Pozieres British Cemetery		40*	1†	81-3-18
Cotton, Pte. I. E., 31390 ...	Merville Communal Cem. Extension	8	F	58	11-8-18
Craggs, Cpl. J., 19982 ...	Memorial in Pozieres British Cemetery		40*	1†	81-3-18
Crampthorn, Pte. G., 38214	Memorial in Dud Corner Cemetery, Loos		62*	1†	24-4-18
Craven, Pte. J. F., 32096	Memorial in Louverval Military Cemetery, Doignies		6*	1†	2-12-17
Creedy, Pte. S. G., 267042	Etretat Churchyard Extension	2	B	8	29-3-18
Critchley, Sgt. E. P., 241215	Tyne Cot Cemetery, Passchendaele (Memorial)		72*	1†	22-8-17
Crocker, Pte. W. F., 44497	Vieille Chapelle New Military Cemetery	5	A	1	24-7-18
Croker, Pte. H. J., 238014	Memorial in Pozieres British Cemetery		40*	2†	25-3-18
Crowley, Pte. M. C., 206425	Memorial in Pozieres British Cemetery		40*	2†	21-3-18
Cull, Pte. A. E., 18546 ...	Hibers Trench British Cem., Wancourt		E	23	7-6-17
Cullingworth, A/Cpl. A. H., 242182	Aval Wood Military Cem., Vieux Berquin	8	E	14	1-9-18
Curtis, Pte. G., 241607 ...	Mont Huon Cemetery, Le Treport	6	F	4A	26-3-18
Curtis, Cpl. W., 241080 ...	Tincourt New British Cem.	4	A	29	7-12-17
Daines, Pte. A., 242084 ...	Memorial in Pozieres British Cemetery		40*	2†	21-3-18
Daniels, Pte. A. J. P., 266170	Aire Communal Cemetery	2	C	29	16-4-18
Darrington, Pte. A., 242109	Memorial in Arras		6*	17†	22-11-17
Dartnell, Pte. W. J., 3195...	Pont du Hem Military Cemetery, La Gorgue	2	A	14	25-9-16
Davey, Pte. G., 290240 ...	Trois Arbres Cemetery, Steenwerck	2	N	21	2-9-18
Davies, Pte. W. H., 242514	Bermerain Communal Cem.		B	8	29-10-18
Davis, Pte. A., 203322 ...	Savy British Cemetery	1	2	20	21-3-18
Davis, Pte. A. J., 18998 ...	Memorial in Dud Corner Cemetery, Loos		62*	1†	18-4-18
Davis, 2nd Lieut. S. A. ...	Memorial in Tyne Cot Cem., Passchendaele		72*	1†	22-8-17
Davis, Cpl. W. G., 1943 (M.M.) ...	Laventie Military Cemetery	2	F	2	19-8-16
Dee, Pte. W. J., 242411 ...	Memorial in Pozieres British Cemetery		40*	2†	31-3-18
Dodgshon, Lieut. A. J. C. ...	Sunken Road Cemetery, Fampoux	1	D	27	10-11-17
Dodwell, Drmr. J. H., 241005	Savy British Cemetery	1	A	2	30-4-17
Dolman, L/Cpl. W., 266797	Memorial in Thiepval				24-4-18
Draisey, Pte. L., 240408 ...	Memorial in Louverval Military Cemetery, Doignies		6*	1†	2-12-17
Drake, L/Cpl. P. C., 242104	Memorial in Louverval Military Cemetery, Doignies		6*	1†	2-12-17

Name	Name of Cemetery or Memorial	Plot	Row	Grave	Date of Death
Driver, Pte. A. E., 242113	... Memorial in Pozieres British Cemetery		40*	2†	81-8-18
Driver, Cpl. C., 242097 (M.M.)	... Vadencourt Military Cem.	1	C	42	7-4-17
Duckett, L/Cpl. J., 266020	... Memorial in Dud Corner Cemetery, Loos		61*	2†	24-4-18
Dulake, Pte. D. H., 242015	... Memorial in Tyne Cot Cem., Passchendaele		73*	2†	4-9-17
English, Pte. W., 5859 ...	... Merville Communal Cem.	6	Q	64	21-6-16
Estcourt, Pte. P. R., 203552	... Memorial in Dud Corner Cemetery, Loos		62*	1†	24-4-18
Eustace, Pte. A., 201592 ...	... Memorial at Thiepval				12-12-17
Evans, Pte. G. J. S., 86264	... Heath Cemetery, Harbonnieres	Special	Memorial		21-3-18
Evans, Pte. G., 265714 ...	... Memorial in Pozieres British Cemetery		40*	2†	81-8-18
Fairbridge, Pte. C. M., 242177	... Calais Southern Cemetery	G	1	14	2-5-17
Faltrick, Pte. A., 235054 ...	... Aire Communal Cemetery	2	F	29	25-4-18
Field, Pte. C., 240480 ...	... Bermerain Communal Cem.	B	5	29-10-18	
Fisher, Pte. L.W., 265946	... Tilloy British Cemetery	1	G	8	3-6-17
Fisher, Sgt. W. H., 242195	... St. Sever Cemetery Extension, Rouen	9 Blk. P	C	13B	8-4-18
Fletcher, Pte. H. J., 201736	... Memorial in Dud Corner Cemetery, Loos		62*	1†	25-4-18
Flint, Pte. A. E., 38271 ...	... Lapugnoy Military Cem.	6	D	4	13-4-18
Fordham, Pte. A. F. M., 3147	... Memorial at Thiepval				22-11-16
Fothergill, Lieut. R. A. ...	... Greenbank Cem., Bristol	PF		182	24-3-18
Fox, Pte. E. J., 200432 ...	... Memorial in Louverval Military Cemetery, Doignies		6*	1†	2-12-17
Francis, L/Cpl. B., 242107	... Memorial in Pozieres British Cemetery		40*	1†	24-3-18
Freeman, Pte. A. J., 31414	... Berlin South West Cem.	5	B	8	1-7-18
Fricker, Pte. F. J., 28496 ...	... Avon View Cem., Bristol	DBK		183	6-5-18
Frost, Pte. E., 267569 ...	... Brandhoek New Military Cemetery	1	E	15	4-9-18
Fudge, Pte. T., 84341 ...	... Memorial in Dud Corner Cemetery, Loos		62*	2†	20-4-18
Furley, Pte. R., 240792 ...	... Villers Bretonneux Military Cemetery	15	F	8	21-8-18
Gainer, Pte. A., 240496 ...	... Poelcapelle British Cemetery	58	D	5	22-8-17
Gale, Lieut. R. G.	... St. Venant Robecq Road British Cemetery, Robecq	4	C	7	24-4-18
Gardner, Pte. H., 241899 (M.M.)	Memorial in Louverval Military Cemetery, Doignies		6*	2†	2-12-17
Gay, Pte. A. J., 260211 ...	... Brandhoek New Military Cemetery	1	C	14	28-8-17
Gay, Pte. S., 201850 ...	... Vieille Chapelle New Military Cemetery	4	F	13	7-4-18
George, Pte. D. T., 88590	... Trois Arbres Cemetery, Steenwerck	2	P	89	2-9-18
Gibson, Pte. A. N., 2981 ...	... Rue-du-Bacquerot No. 1 Military Cem., Laventie	1	L	15	27-7-16
Gilby, Pte. A. V., 242053 ...	... Memorial in Louverval Military Cemetery, Doignies		6*	2†	4-12-17
Glendinning, Pte. H., 201188	... Guemappe British Cemetery	2	B	1	3-6-17
Godsell, L/Cpl. A. C., 8342	... Pont Du Hem Military Cemetery, La Gorgue	2	A	19	25-9-16
Godwin, Pte. A. C., 3165 ...	... Memorial in Dud Corner Cemetery, Loos		62*	2†	24-4-18
Goode, Cpl. S. M., 241288 (M.M.)	Cayeux Military Cemetery	Brit.	C	9	14-4-17

Name	Name of Cemetery or Memorial	Plot	Row	Grave	Date of Death
Gorin, Pte. L., 81403	Memorial in Dud Corner Cemetery, Loos		62*	2†	24-4-18
Gosling, Pte. P. A., 2217	Regina Trench Cemetery, Courcelette	7	A	28	24-12-16
Gratland, L/Cpl. E., 201801 ...	Namps au Val British Cem.	1	G	8	4-4-18
Greasley, Pte. G., 38249	Chapelle British Cemetery	1	D	8	31-3-18
Green, Pte. E., 25683 ...	Memorial in Pozieres British Cemetery		40*	3†	31-3-18
Greenway, Pte. W. H., 202162 ...	Vadencourt British Cem.	1	C	44	7-4-17
Grensted, L/Cpl. C. H., 241870 ...	Cross Roads Cemetery, Fontaine-au-Bois	8	A	4	2-11-18
Grey, L/Sgt. A., 201712	Memorial in Pozieres British Cemetery		40*	1†	31-3-18
Griffin, Pte. F. P., 201642 ...	Awoignt British Cemetery	2	C	20	3-11-18
Griffiths, Pte. A., 203613	Memorial near the Faubourg d'Amiens Cem., Arras		6*	17†	21-6-17
Griffiths, 2nd Lieut. J. E. ...	St. Venant Robecq Road British Cemetery, Robecq	4	C	14	23-4-18
Grindell, Pte. W. E., 260188 ...	Rocquigny Equancourt Rd. British Cemetery	7	C	30	11-12-17
Grist, L/Cpl. R. W. S., 19315 ...	Memorial in Dud Corner Cemetery, Loos		61*	2†	24-4-18
Groves, Sgt. H. W., 20132 (M.M.)	Merville Communal Cem. Extension	1	D	35	11-8-18
Hack, Pte. J. W., 266952	Berguette Churchyard	11	B	1	29-4-18
Hadley, Pte. F., 16714	St. Sever Cemetery Extension, Rouen	Blk. P	C	3B	7-5-18
Hadley, Sgt. J. H., 242404 ...	Savy British Cemetery	1	M	16	21-3-18
Haigh, Pte. H., 200939	Merville Communal Cem. Extension	1	D	36	11-8-18
Hales, Pte. H. T., 202108	Memorial in Tyne Cot Cem., Passchendaele		73*	3†	27-8-17
Hall, Pte. J., 4517	Royal Irish Rifles Graveyard, Laventie	2	J	1	21-6-16
Hancox, Cpl. L. D., 240338 ...	Lijssenthoek Military Cem.	18	B	19	23-8-17
Hanks, L/Cpl. E. B., 241630 ...	Memorial in Tyne Cot Cem., Passchendaele		72*	3†	22-8-17
Harding, Pte. B., 28024	Merville Communal Cem. Extension	1	D	34	11-8-18
Hardman, Sgt. H., 265036 ...	Memorial in Pozieres British Cemetery		40*	1†	31-3-18
Hardwick, L/Cpl. C., 11684 ...	Longuenesse (St. Omer) Souvenir Cemetery	5	D	52	15-8-18
Hardwick, Pte. C., 13673	Memorial in Pozieres British Cemetery		40*	3†	31-3-18
Harrison, L/Cpl. V. C., 241072 ...	Roye New British Cemetery	8	A	15	23-3-18
Harvey, Capt. E. H. (M.C. & Bar)	Estaires Communal Cem. Extension	5	H	1	30-9-18
Haskins, Pte. W. G., 37805 ...	Memorial in Dud Corner Cemetery, Loos		62*	2†	24-4-18
Hawkins, Pte. P. St., 3151 ...	Cheltenham Cemetery	Sect. Q		Grave 10318	9-10-17
Haylock, L/Cpl. T., 242028 ...	Memorial in Pozieres British Cemetery		40*	2†	21-3-18
Hayward, Pte. S., 201194 ...	Memorial in Pozieres British Cemetery		40*	3†	21-3-18
Hazell, L/Cpl. A. W., 201375 ...	St. Venant Communal Cem. Extension		B	40	30-9-18
Hedges, Pte. F. R., 265806 ...	Duisans British Cemetery	6	D	83	16-11-17
Hendy, Pte. L., 34358	Aire Communal Cemetery	4	F	6	18-4-18

Name	Name of Cemetery or Memorial	Plot	Row	Grave	Date of Death
Herbert, Pte. R., 202058	Berlin South Western Cem.	3	B	7	26-6-18
Hewer, Pte. W. E., 34342 ...	Aire Communal Cemetery	4	E	9	2-10-18
Hickman, Pte. J. A., 241856 ...	Vadencourt British Cem.	1	C	46	7-4-17
Hicks, Pte. P. G., 266772	Les Baraques Military Cem.	4	A	13	1-6-18
Higgs, Pte. M. J., 202576	Aire Communal Cemetery	2	E	4	21-4-18
Hill, L/Sgt. J., 25694 ...	Memorial in Pozieres British Cemetery		40*	1†	31-3-18
Hill, Pte. R. V. W., 29273 ...	Memorial in Dud Corner Cemetery, Loos		62*	2†	17-4-18
Hilliard, Pte. G., 266563	Arnos Vale Cem., Bristol	Soldiers Corner	1	679	24-6-18
Hillier, L/Sgt. H., 265167... ...	Royal Irish Rifles Graveyard, Laventie	3	F	10	18-9-18
Hinde, Sgt. H. E., 2397 ...	Laventie Military Cemetery, La Gorgue	2	A	8	30-6-16
Hodder, Pte. G., 201157	Etretat Churchyard Extension	2	D	3	28-4-18
Hodges, Pte. E., 200433	Memorial in Pozieres British Cemetery		40*	3†	31-3-18
Hodges, Pte. G., 241479	Mendinghem Military Cem.	5	A	5	31-8-17
Hodson, Pte. H., 285182	Aire Communal Cemetery	2	H	23	3-5-18
Holdsworth, Pte. W. E., 44498 ...	Vieille Chapelle New Military Cemetery	5	A	2	24-4-18
Holland, Pte. G., 21999 ...	Lillers Communal Cemetery Extension		B	35	17-4-18
Hopes, Pte. S. G., 240420 ...	Aire Communal Cemetery	2	D	22	18-4-18
Hopkins, Pte. W., 202022 ...	Memorial in Berks Cemetery Extension, Ploegsteert		5*	8†	30-9-18
Hornsey, Pte. H. W., 5910 ...	Merville Communal Cem.	11	B	3	17-8-16
Horton, L/Cpl. A. F., 267045 ...	Memorial in Louverval Military Cemetery, Doignies		6*	1†	2-12-17
Hounslow, L/Cpl. J., 241625 ...	Vadencourt British Cem.	1	C	39	7-4-17
Hounsome, Pte. T. E., 241721 ...	Vadencourt British Cem.	1	C	41	7-4-17
Howe, Pte. J. D., 285184	Cardiff Cemetery, South Wales	L	C.E.	2928	28-11-18
Howland, L/Cpl. S. P., 5888 ...	Merville Communal Cem. Extension	1	A	31	20-10-16
Howse, Pte. A., 202503 ...	Memorial in Tyne Cot Cem., Passchendaele		74*	1†	22-8-17
Huckman, Pte. R., 26545 ...	Memorial in Louverval Military Cemetery, Doignies		6*	2†	2-12-17
Hulbert, Pte. E. T., 51710 ...	Abbeville Communal Cem. Extension	5	G	42	18-4-19
Hulett, Cpl. F. G., 5852	Memorial at Thiepval				21-12-16
Humphries, Cpl. S. W. G., (M.M.) 240810	Chapelle British Cemetery	1	F	14	31-3-18
Hunt, Pte. M. H., 3400	Contay British Cemetery	7	B	5	24-12-16
Ind, Sgt. V. F W., 241629 (D.C.M.)	Rocquigny Equancourt Rd. British Cemetery	5	C	4	3-12-17
Ind, Pte. T., 241327 ...	Noordpeene Churchyard				11-8-17
Jackson, Pte. C. W., 3580 ...	Royal Irish Rifles Graveyard, Laventie	2	J	2	21-6-16
Jackson, 2nd Lieut. D. T. ...	Laventie Military Cemetery, La Gorgue	4	D	9	30-9-18
Jackson, 2nd Lieut. J. ...	Laventie Military Cemetery, La Gorgue	2	F	8	19-8-16
James, L/Sgt. G. R., 8279 ...	La Gorgue Communal Cem.	2	C	15	29-6-18
James, Pte. H., 241706 ...	Memorial in Pozieres British Cemetery		40*	3†	23-3-18

Name	Name of Cemetery or Memorial	Plot	Row	Grave	Date of Death
James, Pte. W., 29995	Memorial in Dud Corner Cemetery, Loos		62*	8†	18–4–18
Jarman, Pte. A. E., 14704	Memorial in Dud Corner Cemetery, Loos		62*	8†	24–4–18
Jefferies, Pte. D. R., 204054	Memorial in Pozieres British Cemetery		40*	8†	31–3–18
Jefferies, Pte. E., 266440	Memorial in Berks Cem. Extension, Ploegsteert		5*	8†	2–9–18
Jeffries, Pte. G. H., 241627	Memorial in Tyne Cot Cem., Passchendaele		74*	1†	22–8–17
Jenkins, Sgt. F. J., 240812	Memorial in Tyne Cot Cem., Passchendaele		72*	2†	22–8–17
Jenman, Pte. A., 5097	Longuenesse (St. Omer) Souvenir Cemetery	4	A	56	24–9–16
Johns, Pte. E., 235287	Villers Bretonneux Military Cemetery	15	F	9	21–8–18
Johnson, Pte. F. A., 203374	Namps au Val British Cem.	1	F	21	1–4–18
Johnston, Pte. R. J., 22069	Memorial in Tyne Cot Cem., Passchendaele		74*	1†	22–8–17
Jones, Pte. A. S., 14087	St. Venant Robecq Road British Cemetery	4	C	16	24–4–18
Jones, Pte. G., 241555	St. Sever Cemetery Extension, Rouen	Blk. P1	A	1A	25–4–17
Jones, Pte. J., 267523	Memorial in Dud Corner Cemetery, Loos		62*	8†	25–4–18
Jones, Pte. O. A., 38509	Romeries Communal Cem. Extension	7	E	16	24–10–18
Jones, Pte. T. H., 201778	Bois Guillaume Communal Cemetery Extension	1	C	19b	9–4–18
Jones, Pte. W., 24814	Memorial in Dud Corner Cemetery, Loos		62*	8†	24–4–18
Jones, Sgt. W. H., 265055	Memorial in Pozieres British Cemetery		40*	1†	31–3–18
Kear, Pte. F. G., 266901	Aval Wood Military Cem., Vieux Berquin	1	BB	9	12–8–18
Keeble, Pte. H., 242086	Vermand Communal Cem.	1	A	1	6–4–17
Keedwell, Pte. C. G., 201134	St. Aubert British Cemetery	5	D	9	23–10–18
Kelson, Pte. R. N., 235310	Memorial in Dud Corner Cemetery, Loos		62*	8†	25–4–18
Kemp, Pte. L. G., 241641	St. Cloud Communal Cem.	Div. H.	11	152	20–10–18
Kendall, Pte. W. I., 266710	Memorial in Louverval Military Cemetery, Doignies		6*	2†	2–12–17
Kerton, Pte. F. J., 24903	Memorial in Pozieres British Cemetery		40*	8†	31–3–18
King, Pte. F., 242094	Trois Arbres Cemetery, Steenwerck	2	K	12	1–9–18
King, Pte. L. T., 203496	Memorial in Pozieres Military Cemetery		40*	8†	28–3–18
Kirk, Pte. A., 235260	Memorial in Louverval Military Cemetery, Doignies		6*	2†	8–12–17
Knight, Pte. E., 4967	Aveluy Communal Cem. Extension		L	22	24–12–16
Knight, Sgt. E., 240076	Memorial in Tyne Cot Cem., Passchendaele		72*	2†	22–8–17
Lacey, Sgt. H. C., 240982	Aire Communal Cemetery	2	F	15	24–4–18
Lafford, Pte. J., 2096	Pont du Hem Military Cemetery, La Gorgue	2	A	16	25–9–16
Lake, Lieut. N. G.	Memorial in Pozieres British Cemetery		40*	1†	24–3–18
Lambert, Pte. H. T., 242078	Les Baraques Military Cem.	3	F	7A	1–5–18

Name		Name of Cemetery or Memorial	Plot	Row	Grave	Date of Death
Lambson, Pte. W., 201234	...	Chapelle British Cemetery, Holnon	4	F	16	31-3-18
Lane, Pte. H. W., 12151	...	Rue du Bois Military Cem., Fleurbaix	2	E	8	30-9-18
Lane, Pte. L. F., 44428	...	Memorial in Dud Corner Cemetery, Loos		62*	3†	24-4-18
Lane, Pte. W. E., 44386	...	Cross Roads Cemetery, Fontaine-au-Bois	3	A	16	1-11-18
Lawson, Lieut.- Col. A. B. (D.S.O. & Bar)		St. Venant Robecq Road British Cemetery, Robecq	3	C	12	24-6-18
Lea, Pte. A., 31449	...	Memorial in Louverval Military Cemetery, Doignies		6*	2†	5-12-17
Lees, Pte. F., 235088	...	Memorial in Pozieres British Cemetery		40*	3†	21-3-18
Lees, Pte. R., 44491	...	Aire Communal Cemetery	2	G	6	27-4-18
Liddell, Pte. W. H., 32835	...	Sunken Road Cemetery, Villers Plouich		A	4	5-12-17
Llewellyn, Pte. W., 201518	...	Rue du Bois Military Cem., Fleurbaix	2	D	6	30-9-18
Long, Pte. C. C., 241595	...	Memorial in Pozieres British Cemetery		40*	3†	31-3-18
Long, Pte. E. I., 36254	...	Ham British Cemetery	1	F	7	22-3-18
Loriot, Pte. T. J., 267313	...	Memorial in Louverval Military Cemetery, Doignies		6*	2†	2-12-17
Luff, Pte. G. E., 201171	...	Thiennes British Cemetery	1	F	16	9-8-18
Luxton, Pte. J., 265368	...	St. Venant Robecq Road British Cemetery	4	C	28	30-5-18
McLean, Cpl. W. D., 241656	...	Villers Bretonneux Military Cemetery (Prov.+)	14	A	1	21-3-18
McMahon, L/Cpl. T., 242034	...	Memorial in Dud Corner Cemetery, Loos		61*	2†	24-4-18
McManus, Pte. E., 44438	...	Aire Communal Cemetery	4	A	27	11-8-18
McPhee, Sgt. R., 242568	...	Memorial in Tyne Cot Cem., Passchendaele		7*	2†	22-8-18
Maggs, Pte. W., 201304	...	Laventie Military Cem.	4	D	4	1-10-18
Mander, Pte. O., 17996	...	Memorial in Pozieres British Cemetery		40*	3†	31-3-18
Mann, Pte. R. C., 241293	...	Trois Arbres Cemetery, Steenwerck	2	K	15	1-9-18
Mann, Pte. W. H., 44484	...	Memorial in Dud Corner Cemetery, Loos		63*	1†	24-4-18
Manners, Pte. O. A., 31412	...	Memorial in Pozieres British Cemetery		40*	3†	31-3-18
Margrove, Pte. J. H., 36809	...	Aire Communal Cemetery	4	D	7	5-9-18
Marriott, Pte. C. F., 5790	...	Memorial at Thiepval				24-12-16
Marshall, Pte. A. F., 241904	...	Memorial in Tyne Cot Cem., Passchendaele		74*	2†	22-8-17
Marshall, Pte. H. A., 240925	...	Niederzwehren Cemetery, Germany	2	H	18	24-10-18
Martin, Cpl. T. de Witt, 266498	...	Le Cateau Military Cem.	5	D	19	28-10-18
Martin, Sgt. W. B., 240569	...	New Irish Farm Cemetery, St. Jean-les-Ypres	11	C	4	16-8-17
Martin, Pte. W. L., 267477	...	Chapelle British Cemetery	2	G	13	31-3-18
Matcham, Pte. W. J., 35498	...	Memorial in Dud Corner Cemetery, Loos		63*	1†	24-4-18
Matthews, Pte. W., 260129	...	Memorial in Dud Corner Cemetery, Loos		63*	1†	25-4-18
Maunder, Pte. F., 23290 (M.M.)	...	Esquelbecq Military Cem.	1	B	39	30-4-18
Mead, Pte. H. E., 37398	...	Aire Communal Cemetery	4	C	29	3-9-18

Name	Name of Cemetery or Memorial	Plot	Row	Grave	Date of Death
Meade, 2nd Lieut. C.	Vermand Communal Cem.			1	5–4–17
Mears, Pte. E. E., 265704	Grand Seraucourt British Cemetery	7	E	6	26–3–18
Miles, Pte. C. A., 31441	Aire Communal Cemetery	2	D	24	19–4–18
Miles, Pte. R. J., 265087	Memorial in Dud Corner Cemetery, Loos		63*	1†	24–4–18
Miller, Lieut. F. C.	St. Venant Robecq Road British Cemetery, Robecq	4	C	21	24–4–18
Mills, Pte. A. C., 242316	Roisel Communal Cemetery Extension	1	L	18	2–4–17
Mills, Pte. H. E., 31603	Memorial in Thiepval				24–4–18
Mills, Pte. W. S. C., 240406	Memorial in Pozieres British Cemetery		40*	3†	31–3–18
Milne, Pte. E. R., 242131	Memorial at Arras		6*	18†	22–11–17
Mitchell, Pte. L., 202869	Memorial in Tyne Cot Cem., Passchendaele		74*	2†	27–8–17
Mitchell, Pte. M. H., 202094	Memorial in Tyne Cot Cem., Passchendaele		74*	2†	22–8–17
Mitchell, Pte. R., 265515	Fins New British Cemetery	8	B	11	13–12–17
Mitchell, Pte. S., 202296	Memorial in Louverval Military Cemetery, Doignies		6*	2†	3–12–17
Mitford, Sgt. H. J., 240343	Aire Communal Cemetery	2	E	5	20–4–18
Monger, L/Cpl. J. E., 240984	St. Sever Cemetery Extension, Rouen	Blk. P	K	12b	9–2–18
Moore, Pte. H. H., 37177	Aire Communal Cemetery	2	F	7	23–4–18
Moore, Pte. J., 203565	Selestat Communal Cem.	Brit.	B	5	30–6–18
Morby, Pte. A. W., 38337	Hangard Communal Cem. Extension	2	B	6	31–3–18
Morgan, L/Cpl. G. E., 203503	St. Venant Robecq Road British Cemetery	4	C	22	30–5–18
Morley, Pte. J. P., 44440	Memorial in Berks Cem. Extension, Ploegsteert		5*	9†	11–8–18
Morris, Pte. A. O., 39324	Wimereux Communal Cem.	10	A	8	4–4–18
Morten, Pte. E., 202700	Cross Roads Cemetery, Fontaine-au-Bois	1	H	14	1–11–18
Mortimer, L/Cpl. P., 241718	Villers Bretonneux Military Cemetery	14	A	3	21–3–18
Moule, L/Cpl. W. R., 203561	Hanret Communal Cem.			156	4–11–18
Mullis, Pte. W., 32819	Memorial in Louverval Military Cemetery, Doignies		6*	2†	3–12–17
Murphy, Pte. F. C., 241361	Memorial in Dud Corner Cemetery, Loos		63*	1†	16–4–18
Murray, L/Cpl. E. W., 265454	St. Venant Robecq Road British Cemetery	1	C	1	29–5–18
Murray, C.S.M. W. J., 240818	Memorial in Louverval Military Cemetery, Doignies		6*	1†	2–12–17
Murrell, Pte. O., 4853	Morlancourt British Cem., No. 1		B	4	15–7–16
Murrells, Sgt. A. E., 267290	Merville Communal Cem. Extension	2	D	1	11–8–18
Mustoe, L/Cpl. R., 241064	Memorial in Tyne Cot Cem., Passchendaele		73*	1†	22–8–17
Myson, L/Cpl. G., 202262	Memorial in Dud Corner Cemetery, Loos		61*	2†	24–4–18
Nash, Pte. C., 267109	Etaples Military Cemetery	66	A	21	28–4–18
Nash, Sgt. E. F., 241986 (M.M.)	Thiennes British Cemetery	1	F	17	10–8–18
Neal, Pte. E. J., 204082	Bedford House Cemetery, Enclosure No. 4, Zillebeke	4	D	11	12–9–18
Newman, L/Sgt. V. G., 240948	Memorial in Dud Corner Cemetery, Loos		61*	1†	21–6–16

Name	Name of Cemetery or Memorial	Plot	Row	Grave	Date of Death
Nicholson, Pte. W., 235246	... St. Venant Robecq Road British Cemetery	1	D	8	14-4-18
Norgate, Pte. J. T., 267090	... St. Sever Cemetery Extension, Rouen	Blk. P.9	F	12 B	7-4-18
Norton, L/Cpl. A., 260193	... Cross Roads Cemetery, Fontaine-au-Bois	1	H	18	1-11-18
Norville, Sgt. F. H., 241162	... Vadencourt British Cem.	1	C	40	7-4-17
Notter, Pte. H. V., 267108	... Aval Wood Military Cem., Vieux Berquin	8	A	1	18-8-18
Nunn, Pte. L., 267299 ...	... Memorial in Pozieres British Cemetery	40*		8†	31-3-18
Nunn, Pte. R. H., 202278	... Memorial in Berks Cem. Extension, Ploegsteert	5*		9†	11-8-18
Nurse, 2nd Lieut. R. J. C.	... Memorial in Pozieres British Cemetery	40*		1†	22-3-18
Ollis, L/Cpl. H. C., 265832	... Sunken Road Cemetery, Villers Plouich		A	8	8-12-17
Onions, L/Cpl. A., 16986	... St. Sever Cemetery Extension, Rouen	Blk. P.7	J	10A	27-3-18
Overbury, Pte. T., 29989	... Aire Communal Cemetery	2	F	16	25-4-18
Owen, Pte. J. J., 285177 ...	... Cross Roads Cemetery, Fontaine-au-Bois	1	H	11	2-11-18
Page, Pte. A. E., 241683 ...	... Memorial in Dud Corner Cemetery, Loos	63*		1†	4-9-16
Pallett, Pte. W., 36678 ...	... Memorial in Tyne Cot Cem., Passchendaele	74*		2†	22-8-17
Palmer, Cpl. C. D. A., 242408	... Avon View Cem., Bristol		DBC	46	15-1-19
Palmer, Sgt. J. E., 3552 ...	... Laventie Military Cemetery	2	F	5	23-8-16
Palmer, Pte. R., 20857 ...	... Merville Communal Cem. Extension	2	D	2	11-8-18
Parfitt, Pte. J. J., 14543 ...	... Querenaing Communal Cem.	1	B	7	1-11-18
Parker, Pte. A., 202798 ...	... Memorial in Dud Corner Cemetery, Loos	63*		1†	18-4-18
Parkin, Pte. G. E., 18566 ...	... Trois Arbres Cemetery, Steenwerck	2	F	9	1-9-18
Parrott, Pte. E. A., 242133	... Royal Irish Rifles Graveyard, Laventie	8	F	6	18-9-18
Pascoe, Sgt. A. W., 242422	... Memorial in Pozieres British Cemetery	40*		1†	31-3-18
Pates, Pte. J. H., 241586 ...	... Vieille Chapelle New Military Cemetery	4	A	5	18-4-18
Payne, Pte. F. C., 242138	... Rocquigny Equancourt Rd. British Cemetery	5	D	16	4-12-17
Payne, Cpl. W. S., 200585	... Aval Wood Military Cem., Vieux Berquin	8	E	18	1-9-18
Pearce, Pte. W., 31387 ...	... Memorial in Louverval Military Cemetery, Doignies	6*		2†	5-12-17
Pearce, L/Cpl. W. F. S., 265250	... Memorial in Dud Corner Cemetery, Loos	61*		2†	24-4-18
Pearce, Lieut. W. J. ...	... Villers Plouich Communal Cemetery	Special + A			2-12-17
Pegler, Cpl. A. G., 200804	... Memorial in Louverval Military Cemetery, Doignies	6*		1†	7-12-17
Perry, Pte. A., 265279 ...	... Bermerain Communal Cem.		B	4	28-10-18
Phelps, Pte. H., 202749 ...	... St. Venant Robecq Road British Cemetery	2	B	17	18-4-18
Phipps, Pte. W., 4688 ...	... Royal Irish Rifles Graveyard, Laventie	2	J	6	20-6-18
Piddock, L/Cpl. P., 38749	... Laventie Military Cemetery	4	D	6	1-10-18
Pike, Pte. L. J., 242125 ...	... Lijssenthoek Military Cem.	18	F	14A	4-9-17

184

Name	Name of Cemetery or Memorial	Plot	Row	Grave	Date of Death
Plant, Pte. F., 1759	Laventie Military Cem., La Gorgue	2	A	10	30-6-16
Pontin, L/Cpl. W. T., 241015 ...	Memorial in Pozieres British Cemetery		40*	2†	31-3-18
Pook, Pte. E. J. H., 44452 ...	Memorial in Dud Corner Cemetery, Loos		63*	2†	24-4-18
Powell, Sgt. F. E., 200924 ...	St. Venant Robecq Road British Cemetery	4	F	14	13-4-18
Powers, Pte. F. T., 242324 ...	Chapelle British Cemetery, Holnon	2	A	2	30-4-17
Preston, Pte. F., 5228	Regina Trench Cemetery, Courcelette	7	C	14	22-11-16
Price, Pte. A. G., 202159 ...	Vadencourt British Cem.	1	C	35	7-4-17
Price, Pte. D., 267535 ...	Romeries Communal Cem. Extension	8	C	9	1-11-18
Pruen, Pte. P. W., 240879 (M.M.)	Memorial in Pozieres British Cemetery		40*	3†	31-3-18
Pullin, Pte. A. G., 44456 ...	Memorial in Dud Corner Cemetery, Loos		63*	2†	24-4-18
Radford, L/Cpl. W., 28375 ...	Aire Communal Cemetery	4	F	16	15-4-18
Ratcliffe, Pte. P., 203219 ...	Faubourg D'Amiens Cem.	6	A	22	16-11-17
Read, Cpl. C. G., 242132 ...	Memorial in Pozieres British Cemetery		40*	1†	31-3-18
Redding, Pte. F. E., 21736 ...	Memorial in Louverval Military Cemetery, Doignies		6*	2†	2-12-17
Redman, Pte. W., 288028 ...	St. Venant Robecq Road British Cemetery	1	D	7	14-4-18
Reynolds, Pte. H. R., 1806 ...	Laventie Military Cemetery, La Gorgue	2	B	2	27-6-16
Reynolds, Pte. W., 242137 ...	Memorial in Louverval Military Cemetery, Doignies		6*	2†	2-12-17
Rhodes, Cpl. R. D., 242036 ...	Fouquescourt British Cem.	2	J	4	5-3-17
Rhymer, Pte. W. C., 1866... ...	Laventie Military Cem., La Gorgue	2	B	5	28-6-16
Richards, Pte. E., 18294 ...	St. Venant Robecq Road British Cemetery	1	E	4	10-5-18
Richards, Pte. W. A., 242571 ...	Vis-en-Artois British Cem.	6	H	7	2-6-17
Richardson, Pte. T. D., 242333 ...	Villers Bretonneux Military Cemetery	15	D	8	31-3-18
Rickerby, Capt. J. H. E. (M.C.) ...	Savy British Cemetery (believed to be)	1	U	15	22-3-18
Ricketts, Pte. E. G., 240987 ...	Memorial in Dud Corner Cemetery, Loos		63*	2†	24-4-18
Riley, L/Cpl. T. H., 242335 ...	Awoignt British Cemetery	3	B	23	11-11-18
Rimell, Cpl. R., 241130 ...	Lijssenthock Military Cem.	18	E	14	12-9-17
Roberts, Pte. C. S., 241561 ...	Fins New British Cemetery	2	E	9	2-12-17
Robinson, Pte. H. E., 240904 ...	Heath Cemetery, Harbonnieres	Special	Memorial		21-3-18
Roe, Pte. R., 33206	Memorial in Dud Corner Cemetery, Loos		63*	2†	18-4-18
Rose, Pte. A. L., 241400 ...	Memorial in Louverval Military Cemetery, Doignies		6*	2†	2-12-17
Rowe, Cpl. J., 242390	Vadencourt British Cem.	1	C	36	7-4-17
Rowe, Pte. S. A., 2460	Warloy Baillon Communal Cemetery Extension	5	C	18	21-7-16
Rowing, L/Cpl. R. G., 11811 ...	Memorial in Dud Corner Cemetery, Loos		61*	2†	24-4-18
Ruck, Pte. W. G., 19201 ...	Laventie Military Cemetery	4	D	5	30-9-18
Rugman, Pte. L., 267458 ...	Memorial in Pozieres British Cemetery		40*	3†	21-3-18

Name	Name of Cemetery or Memorial	Plot	Row	Grave	Date of Death
Rumbold, Pte. S. G., 5276	La Neuville Communal Cemetery		B	59	2-2-17
Russell, Pte. G., 240645	Laventie Military Cemetery	4	D	8	30-9-18
Ryan, Pte. J. C., 5765	Rue Du Bacquerot 13th Lond. Graveyd., Laventie		C	21	21-6-16
Sansum, Pte. H. R., 290178	Memorial in Louverval Military Cemetery, Doignies		6*	2†	2-12-17
Saunders, Pte. L. B., 203583	Memorial in Dud Corner Cemetery, Loos		63*	2†	24-4-18
Saunders, Pte. W., 44465	Trois Arbres Cemetery, Steenwerck	2	L	10	2-9-18
Saunders, L/Cpl. W. H., 2128 (M.M.)	Laventie Military Cemetery	2	F	1	19-8-16
Savage, Pte. C. H., 266680	Almondsbury (St. Mary the Virgin) Churchyard	(Not stated)			20-10-18
Savill, Pte. G. H., 82263	St. Venant Robecq Road British Cemetery	2	A	10	19-4-18
Scarrott, Pte. A. E., 260198	Memorial in Pozieres British Cemetery		40*	8†	22-3-18
Scorey, Pte. H., 44466	Memorial in Dud Corner Cemetery, Loos		63*	2†	24-4-18
Scrivener, Pte. A. W., 38413	St. Venant Robecq Road British Cemetery	1	D	6	14-4-18
Searle, L/Cpl. P., 238043	St. Venant Robecq Road British Cemetery	1	F	6	1-5-18
Shergold, Pte. A. B., 266843	Sunken Road Cemetery, Villers Plouich		A	6	7-12-17
Sizeland, Cpl. R. W., 267202	Rue Du Bois Military Cem., Fleurbaix	2	D	1	30-9-18
Skillern, Pte. E., 3345	Royal Irish Rifles Graveyard, Laventie	2	J	4	21-6-16
Skinner, Pte. J. W., 5881	Pont Du Hem Military Cemetery, La Gorgue	1	D	19	31-7-16
Smith, Pte. A. E., 33641	Memorial at Thiepval				27-4-17
Smith, Pte. A. V., 32449	Laventie Military Cemetery	4	D	8	30-9-18
Smith, Pte. C., 38179	St. Venant Robecq Road British Cemetery	1	E	7	19-4-18
Smith, Pte. C. F., 203899	Neuf Brisach Communal Cemetery Extension		7	24	29-6-18
Smith, Pte. E. G., 242336	Vadencourt British Cem.	1	C	34	7-4-17
Smith, Pte. E. H., 201151	Memorial in Pozieres British Cemetery		40*	8†	31-3-18
Smith, Pte. H., 3560	Longuenesse (St. Omer) Souvenir Cemetery	2	C	23	1-7-16
Smith, Pte. J., 17875	Roisel Communal Cemetery Extension	3	L	11	13-1-18
Smith, Pte. J. R., 31798	Rocquigny Equancourt Rd. British Cemetery	5	D	29	6-12-17
Smith, Pte. P. G., 235280	Memorial in Pozieres British Cemetery		40*	8†	31-3-18
Smith, Pte. R. C., 267066	Aire Communal Cemetery	2	F	21	26-4-18
Smith, Sgt. R. D., 240379	Memorial in Louverval Military Cemetery, Doignies		6*	1†	2-12-17
Smith, Pte. W., 44472	St. Venant Robecq Road British Cemetery	1	C	2	29-5-18
Smith, L/Cpl. W. E., 241144	Memorial in Pozieres British Cemetery		40*	2†	31-3-18
Snowden, Cpl. F. J., 242559	Cross Roads Cemetery, Fontaine-au-Bois	1	H	16	1-11-18
Speechley, Pte. A. W. V., 38896	Laventie Military Cemetery	4	D	7	30-9-18
Speed, L/Cpl. S. A., 266077	Memorial in Dud Corner Cemetery, Loos		61*	2†	24-4-18

Name		Name of Cemetery or Memorial	Plot	Row	Grave	Date of Death
Spencer, Pte. J., 241871 ...	...	Vadencourt British Cem.	5	A	13	2-4-17
Sprague, Pte. A. H., 202804	...	Memorial in Dud Corner Cemetery, Loos		63*	3†	24-4-18
Stacey, Pte. R. C., 241632	...	Memorial in Louverval Military Cemetery, Doignies		6*	2†	5-12-17
Stephens, Pte. E., 265246	...	Arnos Vale Cemetery, H.H.N. Bristol			32	24-9-18
Stephens, Cpl. E. L., 3370	...	Merville Communal Cem.	11	B	49	15-7-16
Stevens, Pte. W. J., 265341	...	Memorial in Dud Corner Cemetery, Loos		63*	3†	24-4-18
Stiley, Pte. W. L., 4573 ...	...	Memorial at Thiepval				25-11-16
Stokes, Pte. H., 25347 ...	...	Cross Roads Cemetery, Fontaine-au-Bois	1	H	18	1-11-18
Stone, Pte. F. J. W., 202328	...	Memorial in Tyne Cot Cem., Passchendaele		74*	3†	19-8-17
Stone, Pte. H. H., 260210	...	Memorial in Tyne Cot Cem., Passchendaele		74*	3†	27-8-17
Strawford, Pte. W. H., 23964	...	Cross Roads Cemetery, Fontaine-au-Bois	1	H	15	2-11-18
Stroud, L/Cpl. W. C., 241050	...	Berlin (South Western) Cemetery	1	H	4	21-6-18
Stubbs, Pte. W., 267160 ...	...	Aire Communal Cemetery	2	C	24	14-4-18
Sweeting, Pte. W. G., 200213	...	Cross Roads Cemetery, Fontaine-au-Bois	1	H	19	1-11-18
Symonds, Pte. R. C., 201915	...	Memorial in Pozieres British Cemetery		41*	1†	31-3-18
Tandy, Pte. A., 241519 ...	...	Memorial in Pozieres British Cemetery		41*	1†	23-3-18
Tanfield, Pte. S., 20593 ...	...	Memorial in Louverval Military Cemetery, Doignies		6*	3†	2-12-17
Tanner, Pte. E. J., 2884 ...	...	Laventie Military Cemetery	2	A	11	30-6-16
Tasker, Pte. W. R., 242348	...	Memorial in Louverval Military Cemetery, Doignies		6*	3†	4-12-17
Tattersall, Pte. L., 37678 ...	...	Memorial in Pozieres British Cemetery		41*	1†	30-3-18
Taylor, Pte. C. H., 288031	...	St. Venant Robecq Road British Cemetery	1	E	14	23-4-18
Taylor, Pte. F. W., 201491	...	St. Venant Robecq Road British Cemetery	1	E	15	18-4-18
Taylor, Pte. J., 203224 ...	...	Savy British Cemetery	1	Z	21	31-3-18
Taylor, Pte. J. A., 240937...	...	Memorial in Tyne Cot Cem., Passchendaele		74*	3†	12-9-17
Teagle, Pte. A., 20368 ...	...	Etaples Military Cemetery	20	E	1A	3-12-16
Teek, Pte. F. E., 203521 ...	...	Memorial in Pozieres British Cemetery		41*	2†	31-3-18
Thomas, Pte. H. J., 203522	...	St. Venant Robecq Road British Cemetery	1	B	10	17-6-18
Thompson, Cpl. A. H., 8089	...	Rue Du Bois Military Cem., Fleurbaix	2	D	7	30-9-18
Tilley, Pte. A. J., 241598	...	Memorial at Thiepval				8-3-17
Tittley, L/Cpl. E., 24803	...	St. Venant Robecq Road British Cemetery	2	B	16	18-4-18
Tomlinson, Pte. H., 26859	...	Vieille Chapelle New Military Cemetery	5	E	14	13-4-18
Townsend, Pte. W. L., 266128	...	Memorial in Dud Corner Cemetery, Loos		63*	3†	24-4-18
Townsing, Sgt. S. G., 5780	...	Rue du Bacquerot No. 1 Military Cemetery	1	L	2	24-7-16
Trigg, Pte. F., 240915 ...	...	Memorial in Pozieres British Cemetery		41*	2†	31-3-18

Name	Name of Cemetery or Memorial	Plot	Row	Grave	Date of Death
Tubbs, Capt. S. B.	Memorial in Tyne Cot Cem., Passchendaele		72*	1†	22-8-17
Tucker, Pte. T. C., 267530 ...	Laventie Military Cemetery	4	D	2	30-9-18
Turbeyfield, Cpl. H. A., 242405 ...	Memorial in Tyne Cot Cem., Passchendaele		72*	3†	22-8-17
Turner, Pte. G., 241863	Thiennes British Cemetery	1	F	18	11-8-18
Upton, Pte. A. H., 203376 ...	St. Venant Robecq Road British Cemetery	2	B	12	18-4-18
Ursell, Pte. A., 4500	Memorial in Dud Corner Cemetery, Loos		63*	3†	4-9-16
Vansanten, Pte. S. S., 4915 ...	Laventie Military Cemetery	2	F	13	1-9-16
Veale, L/Sgt. E. E., 266719 ...	Memorial in Dud Corner Cemetery, Loos		61*	1†	2-6-18
Ventris-Field, Pte. B. F., 241032	Cayeux Military Cemetery	British	E	5	4-5-17
Walker, Pte. H., 44484	Memorial in Dud Corner Cemetery, Loos		63*	3†	25-4-18
Walker, Pte. T. W., 44483 ...	Memorial in Dud Corner Cemetery, Loos		63*	3†	25-4-18
Ward, Pte. C. H., 3227	Rue du Bacquerot No. 1 Military Cemetery	2	G	16	2-6-16
Ward, Pte. H., 241559	Memorial in Dud Corner Cemetery, Loos		63*	3†	18-4-18
Waring, Pte. J. W., 38409 ...	Memorial in Louverval Military Cemetery, Doignies		6*	4†	2-12-17
Warner, Pte. E. P., 36357... ...	Cross Roads Cemetery, Fontaine-au-Bois	1	H	12	2-11-18
Warren, Pte. W. A., 241974 ...	Memorial in Pozieres British Cemetery		41*	2†	31-3-18
Wasley, Pte. A. G., 3172	Rue du Bacquerot No. 1 Military Cemetery	1	L	18	27-7-16
Waters, Pte. A. E., 242358 ...	Vadencourt British Cem.	1	C	45	7-4-17
Watkins, L/Cpl. A., 241506 ...	Memorial in Tyne Cot Cem., Passchendaele		73*	1†	22-8-17
Weaver, L/Cpl. W. G., 1855 ...	Memorial at Thiepval				21-12-16
Webb, Pte. A. J., 266717	Memorial in Berks Cem. Extension, Ploegsteert		5*	9†	1-10-18
Webb, Pte. W., 241971	St. Venant Robecq Road British Cemetery	2	E	1	24-4-18
Webb, Pte. W. G., 241270 ...	Upton St. Leonards Churchyard, Glos.			984	25-6-21
Weeks, L/Cpl. A. B., 242122 ...	Duisans British Cemetery	6	D	88	17-11-17
Wentworth, Pte. C. J., 240993 ...	Memorial at Thiepval				28-4-17
Westall, Pte. F. W., 44488 ...	Memorial in Berks Cem. Extension, Ploegsteert		5*	9†	11-8-18
Westbury, Pte. J., 242427 ...	Memorial in Pozieres British Cemetery		41*	2†	31-3-18
Whatley, Pte. P. A., 202216 ...	Vadencourt British Cem.	1	C	43	7-4-17
Wheatcroft, Pte. T., 38408 ...	St. Sever Cemetery Extension, Rouen	Blk. S4	F	8	12-2-19
White, Pte. A. L., 2982	Assevillers New British Cemetery	6	C	4	17-2-17
White, Pte. F. G., 204091 ...	Tincourt New British Cem.	3	E	29	4-12-17
Whitelock, Pte. A. E., 7458 ...	Contay British Cemetery	7	A	22	27-11-16
Whitford, Pte. E., 203524... ...	Romeries Communal Cem. Extension	7	E	12	24-10-18
Wiley, Pte. W., 37970	Cross Roads Cemetery, Fontaine-au-Bois	3	A	2	2-11-18
Wilkins, Cpl. G. E., 241181 ...	Vadencourt British Cem.	1	C	33	7-4-17
Wilkinson, 2nd Lieut. F. W. ...	Rue du Bacquerot No. 1 Military Cem., Laventie	1	L	17	28-7-16

Name	Name of Cemetery or Memorial	Plot	Row	Grave	Date of Death
Williams, Pte. C. E., 260194	Cayeux Military Cemetery	British	E	6/9	27-3-18
Williams, Pte. C. G., 34671	St. Sever Cemetery Extension, Rouen	Blk. S4	F	1	14-2-19
Williams, Pte. W., 5142	Laventie Military Cemetery	2	F	6	24-8-16
Williams, Pte. W., 5768	Merville Communal Cem.	5	B	11	11-7-16
Wilson, Pte. A., 5785	Laventie Military Cemetery	2	E	5	18-7-16
Wilson, Pte. C. H., 44489	Memorial in Dud Corner Cemetery, Loos		61*	2†	24-4-18
Wiltshire, Pte. A., 16727	Villers Bretonneux Military Cemetery	14	D	2	21-3-18
Windsor, Pte. H. J., 4556	Merville Communal Cem. Extension	1	A	18	23-9-16
Witchell, Pte. E. T., 30447	St. Venant Communal Cem. Extension		B	21	2-10-18
Wood, Pte. J., 32862	St. Venant Robecq Road British Cemetery	4	F	15	13-4-18
Woodey, Pte. H. J., 242361	St. Sever Cemetery Extension, Rouen (Blk P)	2	M	2B	22-5-17
Woodhouse, L/Cpl. H., 15086	Grevillers British Cemetery	18	B	7	2-12-18
Woodman, Pte. C., 28174	Memorial in Pozieres British Cemetery		41*	3†	31-3-18
Woodman, Pte. E., 260214	St. Venant Robecq Road British Cemetery	4	C	15	24-4-18
Woodward, Pte. R. H., 240138	Brown's Copse Cemetery, Roeux	4	B	11	15-11-17
Wooles, Pte. G., 204073	Ham British Cemetery, Muille Villette	2	D	4	31-3-18
Woore, Pte. A. C., 240994	Crucifix Corner Cemetery, Villers Bretonneux	9	C	21 (MB)	31-3-18
Workman, L/Cpl. F. Y., 241633	Memorial in Pozieres British Cemetery		40*	2†	31-3-18
Wyatt, 2nd Lieut. J.	Vertain Communal Cem. Extension		C	4	25-10-18
Yardley, Pte. W. R., 3326	St. Venant Robecq Road British Cemetery	1	F	5	1-5-18
Yeldham, Pte. F. G., 5783	Royal Irish Rifles Graveyard, Laventie	2	J	8	21-6-16
Yiend, Pte. J. H. E., 241291	Winchcomb Cemetery, Glos.				8-6-18
Young, Pte. C., 241877	Memorial in Louverval Military Cemetery, Doignies		6*	5†	2-12-17
Young, L/Sgt. F. E., 240115	Memorial in Louverval Military Cemetery, Doignies		6*	1†	2-12-17
Young, Pte. W., 5807	Memorial in Dud Corner Cemetery, Loos		64*	3†	21-6-16
Younger, Pte. A. J., 2251	Memorial at Thiepval				21-12-16

Total killed ... 548
Total wounded ... 1,214

The information contained in the foregoing list has been obtained from the Imperial War Graves Commission and the Editor takes this opportunity of expressing his thanks for the help which he received in compiling the roll.

LIST OF OFFICERS WHO GAINED DISTINCTION WHILE SERVING WITH BATTALION

<table>
<tr><td></td><td></td><td colspan="2">Date of Award or
Gazette</td></tr>
<tr><td>D.S.O.</td><td></td><td></td><td></td></tr>
<tr><td>Lt.-Col. A. B. Lawson</td><td>.. D.S.O. ..</td><td>..</td><td>21 April, 1918</td></tr>
<tr><td></td><td>.. Bar to D.S.O.</td><td>..</td><td>16 September, 1918</td></tr>
<tr><td>Lt.-Col. P. Balfour</td><td>.. D.S.O. ..</td><td>..</td><td>8 June, 1917</td></tr>
<tr><td>Lt.-Col. G. F. Collett</td><td>.. D.S.O. ..</td><td>..</td><td>3 June, 1918</td></tr>
<tr><td>Lt.-Col. G. C. Christie Miller</td><td>D.S.O. ..</td><td>..</td><td>8 March, 1919</td></tr>
<tr><td></td><td></td><td></td><td></td></tr>
<tr><td>M.C.</td><td></td><td></td><td></td></tr>
<tr><td>Capt. E. W. Wales</td><td>.. M.C. ..</td><td>..</td><td>27 July, 1916</td></tr>
<tr><td>Capt. J. H. E. Rickerby ..</td><td>M.C. ..</td><td>..</td><td>22 September, 1916</td></tr>
<tr><td>"</td><td>..Silver Medal for
Military Valour</td><td></td><td>26 March, 1917</td></tr>
<tr><td>Lieut. F. H. L. Varcoe ..</td><td>M.C. ..</td><td>..</td><td>22 September, 1916</td></tr>
<tr><td>Capt. R. S. B. Sinclair ..</td><td>M.C. ..</td><td>..</td><td>18 June, 1917</td></tr>
<tr><td></td><td>.. Bar to M.C.</td><td>..</td><td>2 November, 1918</td></tr>
<tr><td>Lieut. S. A. Pakeman ..</td><td>M.C. ..</td><td>..</td><td>18 June, 1917</td></tr>
<tr><td>Capt. A. F. Barnes</td><td>.. M.C. ..</td><td>..</td><td>1 January, 1917</td></tr>
<tr><td>Capt. J. D. Johnston</td><td>.. M.C. ..</td><td>..</td><td>18 October, 1917</td></tr>
<tr><td>Capt. M. F. Badcock</td><td>.. M.C. ..</td><td>..</td><td>17 December, 1917</td></tr>
<tr><td>Major G. C. Beloe</td><td>.. M.C. ..</td><td>..</td><td>1 January, 1918</td></tr>
<tr><td>Capt. A. Bicknell</td><td>.. M.C. ..</td><td>..</td><td>1 January, 1918</td></tr>
<tr><td>Capt. L. Dudbridge</td><td>.. M.C. ..</td><td>..</td><td>18 February, 1918</td></tr>
<tr><td>"</td><td>.. Bar to M.C.</td><td>..</td><td>24 April, 1918</td></tr>
<tr><td>2nd Lieut. G. W. Radford ..</td><td>M.C. ..</td><td>..</td><td>18 February, 1918</td></tr>
<tr><td>Capt. H. V. Gray ..</td><td>M.C. ..</td><td>..</td><td>26 July, 1918</td></tr>
<tr><td>Capt. T. S. Foweraker ..</td><td>M.C. ..</td><td>..</td><td>3 June, 1918</td></tr>
<tr><td>Lieut. W. H. Horton</td><td>.. M.C. ..</td><td>..</td><td>16 September, 1918</td></tr>
<tr><td>2nd Lieut. P. O. Norton ..</td><td>M.C. ..</td><td>..</td><td>16 September, 1918</td></tr>
<tr><td>Capt. C. E. N. Lavender..</td><td>Bar to M.C.</td><td>..</td><td>1 February, 1919</td></tr>
<tr><td>Capt. E. H. Harvey ..</td><td>Bar to M.C.</td><td>..</td><td>11 January, 1919</td></tr>
<tr><td>2nd Lieut. N. V. Halward ..</td><td>M.C. ..</td><td>..</td><td>1 February, 1919</td></tr>
<tr><td>2nd Lieut. A. Otterburn ..</td><td>M.C. ..</td><td>..</td><td>1 February, 1919</td></tr>
<tr><td>Capt. H. Horton ..</td><td>M.C. ..</td><td>..</td><td>8 March, 1919</td></tr>
<tr><td>2nd Lieut. F. J. Stebbing ..</td><td>M.C. ..</td><td>..</td><td>8 March, 1919</td></tr>
<tr><td>Capt. E. N. Gardner</td><td>.. M.C. ..</td><td>..</td><td>1 January, 1919</td></tr>
</table>

The Editor is indebted to Mr. E. A. Dixon of the Historical Section of the Committee of Imperial Defence for the Honours Lists, which involved considerable search. They are believed to be complete, but in the event of omissions the Editor offers his apologies.

LIST OF OTHER RANKS WHO GAINED
DISTINCTION WHILE SERVING WITH BATTALION

			Date of Award or Gazette
D.C.M.			
3412	Pte. L. Fletcher	.. ..	27 July, 1916
2070	Pte. C. Davies	.. ..	22 September, 1916
1958	Sgt. H. W. Webb ..	.. .. ..	22 September, 1916
241643	Sgt. H. Coleman	.. ..	4 June, 1917
,,	,, M.M. ..	.. ..	26 May, 1917
240069	L/Sgt. F. Davies	.. .. ..	18 June, 1917
241629	Sgt. V. F. W. Ind	.. .. ..	22 October, 1917
38231	Pte. D. Carney	.. .. ..	28 March, 1918
240291	Sgt. H. Wood	.. .. ..	3 June, 1918
240836	Sgt. H. F. Terrett ..	.. .. ..	30 October, 1918
240397	Sgt. E. G. White ..	.. .. ..	3 September, 1918
267293	Cpl. F. A. Elliott ..	.. .. ..	28 March, 1918
12117	Pte. F. F. Fry	.. .. ..	18 February, 1919
36647	L/Cpl. G. E. Harris	.. .. ..	18 February, 1919
241211	Sgt. A. E. Barnes ..	.. .. ..	12 March, 1919
242075	Sgt. E. H. H. Cobbold	.. .. ..	19 March, 1919
,,	,, M.M. ..	.. ..	2 November, 1917
M.M.			
3118	Sgt. A. H. Norris ..	.. .. ..	10 August, 1916
5887	Cpl. C. Driver	.. .. ..	10 August, 1916
1943	Cpl. W. G. Davies	.. .. ..	21 September, 1916
2840	L/Cpl. S. W. G. Humphries	.. ..	21 September, 1916
2270	Pte. F. E. Mundy ..	.. .. ..	21 September, 1916
2248	Pte. W. P. Hester ..	.. .. ..	21 September, 1916
2128	Pte. W. H. Sanders	.. .. ..	21 September, 1916
3045	Pte. J. T. Smith ..	.. .. ..	21 September, 1916
2938	Sgt. A. Howitt	.. .. ..	21 October, 1916
3320	Cpl. A. Hitchman	.. .. ..	21 October, 1916
3086	Pte. C. J. Arkell ..	.. .. ..	21 October, 1916
3168	Pte. W. R. Stanbridge	.. .. ..	21 October, 1916
2964	Pte. C. V. Spillard	.. .. ..	21 October, 1916
241288	Cpl. S. M. Goode	.. .. ..	17 April, 1917
241134	Pte. H. C. Barnfield	.. .. ..	2 November, 1917
203053	L/Cpl. B. W. Ensor	.. .. ..	2 November, 1917
241899	Pte. H. W. Gardner	.. .. ..	2 November, 1917
241813	Pte. D. McCafferty	.. .. ..	2 November, 1917
241986	L/Sgt. E. F. Nash ..	.. .. ..	2 November, 1917
240932	Dmr. C. R. Pearce	.. .. ..	2 November, 1917
240879	Pte. P. D. Pruen ..	.. .. ..	2 November, 1917
241178	Pte. F. C. Weaver ..	.. .. ..	2 November, 1917
241682	Pte. J. F. Gegg ..	.. .. ..	19 November, 1917
241551	Cpl. F. Williams ..	.. .. ..	28 January, 1918
22273	Pte. C. H. Hoskins	.. .. ..	28 January, 1918
26081	Pte. E. Gomme ..	.. .. ..	28 January, 1918
235292	Pte. E. G. Clutterbuck	.. .. ..	23 February, 1918
200325	Sgt. H. W. Porter ..	.. .. ..	23 February, 1918
201080	Pte. W. Doydge ..	.. .. ..	23 February, 1918
201652	Sgt. J. Fox	.. .. ..	23 February, 1918
202868	Cpl. S. M. Santer ..	.. .. ..	23 February, 1918

<table>
<tr><td colspan="2">M.M. (cont.)</td><td>Date of Award or Gazette</td></tr>
</table>

30587	Sgt. W. Craner .. (and Bar)	.. 23 February, 1918
16460	Pte. W. J. Harper	.. 23 February, 1918
200329	Pte. J. Abrahams	.. 13 March, 1918
241626	Pte. W. A. Davis	.. 13 March, 1918
265821	Pte. J. E. Kilminster	.. 13 March, 1918
266640	Pte. H. T. Tiley	.. 13 March, 1918
265102	Cpl. J. Gapper	.. 10 April, 1918
241380	Pte. H. Palmer	.. 12 June, 1918
241006	L/Cpl. F. Elliott	.. 27 June, 1918
201201	Cpl. G. Hall	.. 27 June, 1918
242377	L/Cpl. C. O. Meates	.. 27 June, 1918
267294	L/Sgt. H. Evans	.. 27 June, 1918
241039	Pte. S. Long	.. 27 June, 1918
241118	Pte. A. R. Price	.. 27 June, 1918
38198	Pte. G. W. H. Blatherwick ..	.. 27 June, 1918
33645	Pte. G. W. Gallow	.. 27 June, 1918
15925	Pte. G. J. Mabbett	.. 27 June, 1918
241157	Pte. E. A. Jones	.. 16 July, 1918
241579	Pte. A. V. Sindrey	.. 16 July, 1918
241186	L/Cpl. A. M. Green	.. 29 August, 1918
241986	Sgt. E. F. Nash .. (and Bar)	.. 7 October, 1918
241626	Cpl. W. A. Davis .. (and Bar)	.. 7 October, 1918
267194	Sgt. S. Skipper .. (and Bar)	.. 7 October, 1918
240897	Sgt. P. H. Brown	.. 7 October, 1918
285937	Pte. W. Davis	.. 7 October, 1918
240946	Cpl. G. S. Gardner	.. 7 October, 1918
267385	Pte. H. G. Jones	.. 7 October, 1918
266762	Cpl. A. G. Turner	.. 7 October, 1918
201060	Sgt. R. H. Livings	.. 11 December, 1918
267491	Pte. A. Barrett	.. 11 December, 1918
267019	Pte. T. Kendall	.. 11 December, 1918
38263	Pte. A. Wileman	.. 11 March, 1919
23795	L/Cpl. C. Willmot	.. 11 March, 1919
265497	Cpl. C. W. Cooper	.. 11 March, 1919
2091	Pte. A. R. Buck	.. 13 March, 1919
37293	L/Cpl. J. R. Newton	.. 13 March, 1919
203090	Cpl. A. H. Harrison	.. 13 March, 1919
242106	Cpl. W. Overton	.. 13 March, 1919

M.S.M.

266199	Cpl. C. J. F. Doel	.. 17 June, 1918
201701	C.S.M. J. W. Fifield	.. 17 June, 1918
266113	C.Q.M.S. W. Farquharson ..	.. 17 June, 1918
202868	Cpl. S. M. Santer	.. 17 June, 1918
242003	C.Q.M.S. A. Gilbert	.. 11 March, 1919
240783	Sgt. T. H. Cater	.. 11 March, 1919

Croix de Guerre.

5802	R.S.M. W. W. Spragg	.. 12 July, 1918
200009	C.S.M. C. H. Andrews	.. 12 July, 1918
241469	L/Sgt. H. F. Wilson	.. 12 July, 1918
267156	C.S.M. S. Lockwood	.. 12 July, 1918

Medal Militaire.

240069	L/Sgt. F. Davies	.. 14 July, 1917

Italian Bronze Bar.

202958	Sgt. A. Oakley	.. 12 September, 1918

www.ingramcontent.com/pod-product-compliance
Lightning Source LLC
Chambersburg PA
CBHW030406100426
42812CB00028B/2847/J